Prayer

CH Spurgeon

WHITAKER
HOUSE

Unless otherwise indicated, all Scripture quotations are taken from the *King James Version* (KJV) of the Holy Bible.

Editor's note: This book has been edited for the modern reader. Words, expressions, and sentence structure have been updated for clarity and readability.

PRAYER
(previously titled *The Golden Key of Prayer*)

ISBN: 0-88368-562-0
Printed in the United States of America
© 1995 by Whitaker House

Whitaker House
30 Hunt Valley Circle
New Kensington, PA 15068
web site: www.whitakerhouse.com

Library of Congress Cataloging-in-Publication Data

Spurgeon, C. H. (Charles Haddon), 1834–1892.
  [Golden key of prayer]
  Prayer: / by Charles Spurgeon.
    p. cm.
Originally published: The golden key of prayer. Springdale, PA : Whitaker House, ©1995.
  ISBN 0-88368-562-0 (trade paper)
  1. Devotional literature, English. 2. Prayers. I. Title.
BV4832.2 .S76 2000
242—dc21
                                        99-087842

2 3 4 5 6 7 8 9 10 11 12 / 10 09 08 07 06 05 04 03 02

Contents

1

Help from On High

You who are King of Kings and Lord of Lords, we worship You. "Before Jehovah's awful throne, we bow with sacred joy." We can truly say that we delight in God. There was a time when we feared You with the fear of bondage. Now we reverence You, but we love as much as we reverence. The thought of Your omnipresence was once horrible to us. We said, *"Whither shall* [we] *flee from thy presence?"* (Psalm 139:7). It seemed to make hell itself more dreadful, because we heard, *"If I make my bed in hell, behold, thou art there"* (v. 8).

But now, O Lord, we desire to find You. Our longing is to feel Your presence, and it is heavenly that You are there. The sick bed is soft when You are there. The furnace of affliction grows cool when You are there. The house of prayer when You are present is none other than the house of God, the very gate of heaven.

Come near, our Father, to Your children. Some of us are very weak in body and faint in heart. Soon, God, lay Your right hand on us and say, "Fear not." Perhaps the world is attracting some of us. Come near to kill the influence of the world with Your superior power. Even to worship may not seem easy to some. The Dragon seems to pursue them, and the floods out of his mouth wash away their devotion. Give them great wings like those of an eagle, so that each may fly away into the place prepared for him, and rest in the presence of God today.

Father, come and give rest to Your children. Take the helmet from our brow. Remove from us the weight of our heavy armor for a while. May we have perfect peace and be at rest. Oh, help us now, we pray. As You have already washed Your people in the fountain filled with blood and they are clean, now wash us from defilement in the water. With the basin and with the pitcher, O Master, wash our feet again. Your cleansing will greatly refresh us. It will prepare us for innermost fellowship with You. For this reason, the priests washed themselves before they went into the Holy Place.

Lord Jesus, now take from us everything that would hinder the closest communion with God. Any wish or desire that might hamper us in prayer, please remove it, Lord. Any memory of sorrow or care that might hinder the fixing of our affection wholly on our God, take it away now. What do we have to do with idols any more? You have seen and observed us.

You know where the difficulty lies. Help us against it, and may we now come boldly, not into the Holy Place only, but into the Holiest of All, where we would not dare come if our great Lord had not rent the veil, sprinkled the mercy seat with His blood, and invited us to enter.

Now we have come close to You, to the light that shines between the wings of the cherubim. We speak with You now as a man speaks with his friend. Our God, we are Yours. You are ours. We are now concerned with one business; we are united together for one battle. Your battle is ours, and our fight is Yours. Help us, we pray. You who strengthened Michael and his angels to cast out the Dragon and his angels, help poor flesh and blood, so that to us also this word may be fulfilled: *"The God of peace shall bruise Satan under your feet shortly"* (Romans 16:20).

Our Father, we are very weak. Worst of all, we are very wicked if left to ourselves, and we soon fall prey to the enemy. Therefore, help us. We confess that sometimes in prayer when we are nearest to You, at that very time some evil thought comes in, some wicked desire. Oh, what poor simpletons we are. Lord, help us. We want to come closer to You still and hide *"under the shadow of* [Your] *wings"* (Psalm 17:8). We wish to be lost in God. We pray that You may live in us, and that it may not be us who live, but Christ in us (Galatians 2:20), showing Himself in and through us. Lord, sanctify us. Oh, may Your spirit come and saturate every faculty, subdue every passion, and use every power of our nature for obedience to God!

Come, Holy Spirit. You have often overshadowed us. Come, and more fully take possession of us. As we feel we are standing now right at the mercy seat, our very highest prayer is for perfect holiness, complete consecration, entire cleansing from all evil. Take our hearts, our heads, our hands, our feet, and use all of us for You. Take our substance; let us not hoard it or spend it for ourselves. Take our talents; let us not educate ourselves so that we may have the reputation of being wise, but let every mental gain be for the purpose of serving You better.

May every breath be for You. May every minute be spent for You. Help us to truly live while we live. And while we are busy in the world as we must be, for we are called to be diligent, may we sanctify the world for Your service. May we be lumps of salt in the midst of society. May our spirits and dispositions, as well as our conversations, be heavenly. May there be an influence about us that will make the world better before we leave it. Lord, hear us in this thing.

And now that we have Your ear, we pray for this poor world in which we live. We are often horrified by it. Lord, for our own comfort, we wish that we did not know anything about it. We have said, "Oh, for a cabin in some wilderness." We hear of oppression, robbery, and murder, and men seem to be let loose against each other. Lord, have mercy on this great and wicked world. What is to be done with these billions? What can we do? At least help every child of Yours to do his utmost. May none of us contribute to the evil directly or indirectly, but may we contribute to the good that is in it.

When Your servant Abraham stood before You and spoke with such wonderful familiarity to You, he pleaded for Sodom. We want to follow the example of the Father of the Faithful; we plead for our city, for all great cities, and indeed for all nations. Lord, let Your kingdom come. Send forth Your light and Your truth. Chase the old Dragon from his throne, with all his hellish crew. Oh, that the day would come when even on earth the Son of the woman, the Man-child, will rule the nations, not with a broken staff of wood, but with an enduring scepter of iron, full of mercy, but full of power, full of grace, and irresistible! Oh, that the advent of our Lord would soon come! We long for the millennial triumph of His Word.

Until then, O Lord, gird us for the fight, and make us to be among those who overcome through the blood of the Lamb and through the word of our testimony, who do not love their lives to the death (Revelation 12:11).

We also lift our voices to You in prayer for all our dear ones. Lord, bless the sick, and

PRAYER

make them well as soon as it is the right time
for them to be well. Sanctify to them all that
they have to bear. There are also dear friends
who are very weak, some who are even trembling. God, bless them. While the tent is being
taken down, may the inhabitant within look on
with calm joy, for before long we will *"be
clothed upon with our house which is from
heaven"* (2 Corinthians 5:2).

Lord, help us to be very loosely attached to
all these things here below. May we live here
like strangers and make the world not a house,
but an inn in which we dine and lodge, expecting to be on our journey tomorrow.

Lord, save the unconverted, and bring out
from among them those who are converted but
who have not confessed Christ. May the
church be built up by many who, having believed, are baptized in the sacred name. We
pray that You will multiply the faithful in the
land. Turn the hearts of men to the Gospel
again! Your servant is often very heavy in heart
because of the departures from the faith. Bring
the wandering back. Do not let Satan take
away any more stars with his tail, but may the
lamps of God shine brightly. You who walk
among the seven golden candlesticks (Revelation 1:12–18), trim the flame, pour forth the oil,
and let Your light shine brightly and steadily.

We leave a broken prayer at the mercy seat
with this at the end of it: we ask in the name of
Jesus Christ, Your Son. Amen.

2

Thanks Be unto God

Lord God, help us now to really worship You. We bless Your name for setting us apart now and always. Lord, will You shut the door on the world for us? Help us to forget our cares. Enable us to rise far above this world. May we get rid of all its tendencies to drag us down. May the attractions of these crude things be gone, and may You catch us away to Yourself.

We do not ask to be entranced or to see an angel in shining apparel, but we do ask that by faith we may see Jesus. May His presence be so evidently realized among us that we may rejoice as well as if our eyes beheld Him. May we love, trust, and worship Him as earnestly as we would if we could now put our fingers into the print of the nails.

Oh, precious Lord Jesus Christ, we do adore You with all our hearts. You are Lord of all. We bless You for becoming man so that You might be our next of kin. Being next of kin, we bless You for taking us into marriage union with Yourself and for redeeming us and our inheritance from the captivity into which we were sold. You have paid Your life for us. You have ransomed Your people with Your heart's blood. Be, therefore, forever beloved and adored.

Now You are not here, for You are risen. Our souls want to track the shining way by which You have ascended through the gate of pearl up to Your Father's throne. We seem to see You sitting there, man, yet God, reigning over all things for Your people. Our ears almost catch the accents of the everlasting song that rolls up at Your feet: *"Worthy is the Lamb that was slain to receive power, and riches, and wisdom, and strength, and honour, and glory, and blessing"* (Revelation 5:12). Lord, we say, "Amen." From the outskirts of the crowd that surrounds Your throne, we lift up our feeble voices in earnest, for You were slain and have redeemed us to God by Your blood and have made us kings and priests unto God (Revelation 1:6). We will reign with You, for though we are far away in terms of physical distance, we know that we are very near to Your heart.

You look over the heads of the angelic squadrons to behold us, and You hear the praises and the groans of Your well beloved. Are we not most near You, Your flesh and Your bones? We know we are. We feel the ties of kinship within us. We are our Best Beloved's, and He is ours. We are longing to move through the crowd that surrounds Him and to get to the forefront. There we would bow prostrate at the dear feet that were nailed to the tree for us, and worship the Lamb who lives forever and ever, who has prevailed to take the book and loose the seven seals thereof (Revelation 5:5), to whom be glory, world without end. Hallelujah!

O Savior, accept these poor praises of ours. They come from those You love. And as we prize all little things that come from those we love, we feel that You will accept the thanksgiving, the reverential homage of Your own redeemed ones who are a people near unto You, whose names are engraved on the palms of Your hands (Isaiah 49:16), of whom You are the active Head, and for whom Your heart beats true and full of love even now.

Oh, we can say we love You. We wish we loved You more, but You are very dear to us. There is none on earth like You. For the love of Your name, we would live and die. If we think we love You more than we do, we pray that we may yet love You more than we think. Oh, take these hearts and unite them with Your own, and be heart and soul and life and everything to us. For *"whom have* [we] *in heaven but thee? and there is none upon earth that* [we] *desire beside thee"* (Psalm 73:25).

We worship the Father, we worship the Son, and we worship the Holy Spirit with all the powers of our being. We fall prostrate before the fearful yet glorious throne of the Infinite Majesty of heaven. May the Lord accept us as we offer these praises in the name of Jesus.

Now, blessed Lord, look down upon those who do not love You. Redeemer, look on them with those eyes of Yours that are as flames of fire. Let them see how badly they treat You. May they consider how dire is their ingratitude that can be negligent of a Savior's blood, indifferent to a Savior's heart. Oh, bring the careless and the godless to seek for mercy. Let those who are delaying serious things begin to see that the very thought of postponement of the claims of Christ is treason against His Majesty. Savior, dart Your arrows abroad and let them wound many so that they may fall down before You and cry for mercy.

But there are some who are wounded. There are broken hearts that seek peace— men and women, like Cornelius, who want to hear the words that God commands. Oh, come, divine Physician, and bind up every broken bone. Come with Your sacred salve that You have made with Your own heart's blood. Apply it to the wounded conscience, and let it feel the balm's power. Give peace to those whose consciences are like the troubled sea that cannot rest.

O God, our God, do not let the teaching of the Sunday school, the preaching of the evangelists, the personal visitations of individuals, do not let any of these efforts be in vain. Do give conversions. We groan out this prayer from our very hearts. Yet we can also sing it, for You have heard us liberally already, and our hearts rejoice in God the Savior who works so graciously among the children of men.

We have been astonished as the Holy Spirit has fallen even on the chief of sinners, and men far from God have been brought in. But, Lord, do more of this among us. Let us see even greater things. Where we have had one saved, let us have a hundred, to the praise of the glorious name of the Beloved.

Lord, keep us all from sin. Teach us how to walk wisely. Enable us to guard our minds against error of doctrine, our hearts against wrong feelings, and our lives against evil actions. Oh, may we never speak unadvisedly with our lips or give way to anger. Above all, keep us from covetousness, which is idolatry, and from malice, which is of the Devil. Grant unto us to be full of sweetness and light. May love dwell in us and reign in us. May every man look not only on his own things, but also on the things of others (Philippians 2:4). Lord, allow us to live for Jesus. There is no life like it. Help us to be Christlike men, Christ's men, and may we in all things reflect the light that we receive from Him.

Lord, prosper all the churches of Jesus Christ. Bless our beloved churches and all their organizations. O God, take care of them.

Make every member of every church a pastor over others. Let all strive together for the good of all, and so may Your kingdom come among us. Let missionaries especially be helped by Your Spirit. May there come a day in which the minds of men may be better prepared to receive the Gospel.

May Messiah's kingdom come to the overthrow of her who sits on the Seven Hills and to the eternal waning of Mohammed's moon, to the overthrow of every idol, so that Christ alone may reign. Our whole hearts cry out for this. Reign, Emmanuel, reign. Sit on the high throne. Ride on Your white horse, and let the armies of heaven follow You, conquering and to conquer. Come, Lord Jesus. Even so, come quickly (Revelation 22:20).

3

Love without
Measure or End

ord, we want to come to You, but may You come to us. Draw us, and we will run after You. Blessed Spirit, help our infirmities, *"for we know not what we should pray for as we ought"* (Romans 8:26). Come, Holy Spirit, and give right thoughts and right words so that we may all be able to pray with other Christians in united, common prayer. Then may everyone in the group feel that there is a portion for each of them. We are grateful as we remember that if our ministers are for some reason unable to pray for us individually, there is One who bears the names of all His redeemed upon His breast and upon His shoulder, who will take care with the love of His heart and the power of His arm to maintain the cause of all His own.

Dear Savior, we put ourselves under Your sacred patronage. Plead for us with the Father, plead for us this day—yes, make intercession for the transgressors. We desire to praise the name of the Lord with our whole hearts. So many of us *"have tasted that the Lord is gracious"* (1 Peter 2:3). Truly You have delivered us from the gulf of dark despair, where we wretched sinners had lain. You have brought us *"up also out of an horrible pit, out of the miry clay, and set* [our] *feet upon a rock"* (Psalm 40:2). The new song that You have put into our mouths (v. 3) we do not want to stifle; we want to bless the Lord whose mercy endures forever.

We thank You, Lord, for the love without beginning that chose us before the earth ever was, for the love without measure that entered into covenant for our redemption, for the love without failure that in due time appeared in the person of Christ and worked out our redemption, for the love that has never changed, though we have wandered, for the love that remains faithful even when we are unfaithful.

O God, we praise You for keeping us until this day, and for the full assurance that You will never let us go. Some can say, *"He restoreth my soul"* (Psalm 23:3). They had wandered, wandered sadly, but You have brought them back again. Lord, keep us from wandering. Then we will sing, *"Unto him that is able to keep* [us] *from falling, and to present* [us] *faultless before the presence of his glory with exceeding joy"* (Jude 24). Bless the Lord, our inmost souls, bless the Lord. Blessed be the

Father, the Son, and the Holy Spirit, the triune God. Blessed be the Lord for every office sustained by each divine person, and for the divine blessing that has come streaming down to us through each one of those gracious titles worn by the Father, Son, and Holy Spirit.

We feel like singing all the time. We want to take down our harps from the willows, if we have hung them there, and we want to awaken every string to the sweetest melody of praise unto the Lord our God. Yet, Lord, we cannot continue to praise You right now, for we are obliged to come before You with humble confession of sin. We are not worthy of the least of these favors. We cannot say, "Because we are worthy, You should do this thing." No, we are altogether unworthy, and Your gifts are according to the riches of Your grace, for which again we praise You.

Lord, forgive us all our sins. May Your pardoned ones have a renewed sense of their acceptance in the Beloved. If any cloud has risen to hide You from any believing eye, take that cloud away. If in our march through this world, so full of mire as it is, we have any spot on us, dear Savior, wash our feet in that blessed footbath, and then say to us, "[You are] *clean every whit*" (John 13:10). May we know that there is no condemnation, no separation. May we know that sin is removed as to its separating as well as its destroying power. And may we enter into full fellowship with

19

God. May we walk in the light as God is in the light, and have fellowship with Him, while the blood of Jesus Christ, His Son, cleanses us from all sin (1 John 1:7). Let no child of Yours have any dead work on his conscience, and may our consciences be purged from dead works to serve the living and true God.

If there are any that, after having made the profession of faith, have gone astray by any form of sin, Lord, restore them. If they have fallen by strong drink, if they have fallen by unchastity, if they have fallen by dishonesty, if, in any way, they have stained their garments, oh, may Your mighty grace bring them back and put them yet among the children. Do not give them up; do not make them like Admah and Zeboim (Deuteronomy 29:23). But let Your sympathy be kindled and Your bowels of compassion be moved for them. Let them also be moved, and may they return with weeping and with supplication and find You a God ready to pardon.

Furthermore, this day we ask of You, our Father, to perfect Your work within our hearts. We are saved, but we want to be saved from sin of every form and degree—from sins that lie within, but we are scarcely aware that they are there. If we have any pride of which we are not conscious, any unbelief of which we are not aware, if there is a clinging to the creature, a form of idolatry that we have not yet perceived, we ask You, Lord, to search us with Your light until You spy out the evil and then put it away. We are not satisfied with pardoned sin. We pray, *"Create in me a clean heart, O God; and renew a right spirit within me"* (Psalm 51:10). Help us in our daily lives, in our families, in our relationships as husbands or wives, parents or children, masters or servants, in our business transactions with our fellowmen, in our dealings with the church of God. May we be true, upright, pure—kept from the great transgression because we are kept from the minor ones.

Oh, may we be among those who glorify Christ. We pray that You will save us from the common religion. Give us the special grace of a special people. May we abide in Christ. May we live near to God. Do not let the frivolities of the world have any power over us whatsoever. May we be too full grown in grace to be bewitched by the toys that are suitable only for children. Oh, lead us to serve You.

Especially—this prayer we have already prayed, but we pray it again—make us useful in the salvation of our fellowman. O Lord, have we lived so long in the world, and yet are our children unconverted? May we never rest until they are truly saved. Have we been going here and there in business, and are those around us still unaware of our Christian character? Have we never spoken to them the Word of Life? Lord, arouse us to a deep concern for all with whom we come in contact from day to day. Make us all missionaries in the home or in the street or in the workplace, wherever Providence has cast our lot. May we there shine as lights in the world.

Lord, keep us right—true in doctrine, true in experience, true in life, true in word, true in deed. Let us have an intense agony of spirit concerning the many who are going down to the everlasting fire of which our Master spoke. Lord, save them! *Lord, save them!* Stop, we pray, the torrents of sin that run down the streets of our cities. Purge the dead sea of sin, in which so many of the heathen are lying. Oh, that the day would come when the name of Jesus is a household word, when everybody knows of His love, of His death, of His blood, and of its cleansing power. Lord, save men; gather the company of the redeemed people. Let those whom the Father gave to Christ be brought out from among the ruins of the Fall to be His joy and crown. *"Let the people praise thee, O God; let all the people praise thee"* (Psalm 67:3). Let the ends of the earth fear Him who died to save them. Let the whole earth be filled with the glory of God.

This is our great prayer, and we crown it with this: come, Lord Jesus, come, Lord, and do not wait! Come in the fullness of Your power and the splendor of Your glory! Come quickly. Even so, come quickly, Lord Jesus (Revelation 22:20).

4

The All-Prevailing Plea

ord God, the Fountain of all fullness! We, who are nothing but emptiness, come unto You for all supplies. We know we do not come in vain, since we bring with us a plea that is all-prevailing. Since we come commanded by Your Word, encouraged by Your promise, and preceded by Christ Jesus, our Great High Priest, we know that whatsoever we ask in prayer, believing, we will receive (Matthew 21:22). May You help us now to ask right things, and may the words of our mouths be acceptable in Your sight, O God, our Strength and our Redeemer (Psalm 19:14).

First, we want to adore Your blessed and ever beloved name. All the earth worships You, the everlasting Father. Heaven is full of Your glory. May men's hearts also be filled with glory unto You. The noblest creatures You have made, whom You set in Paradise, for whom the Savior shed His blood, may they love You with all their hearts.

The faithful—chosen, called, and separated—join in the everlasting song. All Your redeemed praise You, O God! As the God of our election, we extol You for Your everlasting and immutable love. As the God and Father of our Lord Jesus Christ, we bless You for that unspeakable gift, the offering of Your Only Begotten. Words are but air, and our tongues but clay. Your compassion is divine. Therefore, it is not possible that any words of ours should sound forth Your worthy praise for this superlative deed of grace.

We bless You, also, divine Son of God, coequal and coeternal with the Father, that You did not disdain to be born of the Virgin, and that, being found in fashion like a man, You did not refuse to be *"obedient unto death, even the death of the cross"* (Philippians 2:8). Let Your brow be adorned with something better than thorns; let the eternal diadem forever glitter there. You were slain and have redeemed us to God by Your blood (Revelation 5:9). Unto You be glory, honor, power, majesty, dominion, and might, forever and ever!

Equally, most blessed Spirit, You who brooded over chaos and brought it into order, You who begot the Son of God's body of flesh, You who quickened us to spiritual life, by whose divine energy we are sanctified and hope to be made *"partakers of the inheritance of the saints in light"* (Colossians 1:12), unto You, also, be hallelujahs, world without end!

O Lord, our souls long for words of fire, but we cannot reach them! Oh, when will we be rid of these clay vessels, which are now so uncongenial to our song? When will we be able with wings to mount upward to Your throne? And having learned some flaming sonnets that have once been sung by cherubim above, when will we be able to praise You forever?

Even these flaming sonnets are not rich enough for Your glory. We want to sing to You a new song. We will, when we reach the heavenly shore, become leaders of the eternal music. Day without night, we will circle God's throne rejoicing, and count it the fullness of our glory, our bliss, our heaven, to wave the palm and cast our crowns with our songs at Your feet forever and ever!

Our Father in heaven, next to this we want to offer prayer for those who never think of You; who, though created by You, are strangers to You; who are fed by Your bounty and yet never lift their voices to You, but live for self, for the world, for Satan, for sin. Father, these cannot pray for themselves because they are dead. Your awakened children pray for them. These will not come to You, for, like sheep, they are lost; but may You seek them, Father, and bring them back.

Our glorious Lord, You have taught us to pray for others, for the grace that met with such undeserving sinners like us must be able to meet with the vilest of the vile. Oh, we cannot boast of what we are. We cannot boast of what we have been by nature. If we had had our doom, we would now be in hell. If this day we had our proper, natural, and deserved position, we would still be *in the gall of bitterness, and in the bond of iniquity*" (Acts 8:23). It is Your rich, free, sovereign, distinguishing grace that has brought us up out of the miry clay and has set our feet upon a rock (Psalm 40:2). And will we even refuse to pray for others? Will we leave a stone unturned for their conversion? Will we not weep for those who have no tears and cry for those who have no prayers? Father, we must and we will.

> Fain our pity would reclaim,
> And snatch the firebrands from the flame.

There are those who are utterly careless about divine things. Will You impress them? May some stray shot reach their consciences! Oh, that they may be led to solemnly consider their position and their latter end! May thoughts of death and of eternity dash irresistibly against their souls like some mighty waves! May heaven's light shine into their consciences! May they begin to ask themselves where and what they are, and may they be turned to the Lord with full purpose of heart.

There are others who are concerned, but they are wavering between two opinions. There are some whom we love in the flesh who have not yet decided for God. Behold, they tremble in the balance! Cast in Your cross, O Jesus, and turn the scale! Love irresistible, come forth, and carry by blessed storm the hearts that have not yet yielded to all the attacks of the law! May some who never could be melted, even by the furnace of Sinai, be dissolved by the beams of love from the tearful eyes of Jesus!

Lord, if there is a heart that is saying, "Now, behold, I yield. At Your feet, rebellion's weapons I lay down and cease to be Your foe, O King of Kings"—if there is one who is saying, "I am willing to be espoused unto Christ, to be washed in His blood, to be called in His righteousness"—bring that willing sinner in now! May there be no more delay, but may this be the time when, once for all, the great transaction will be done, and they will be their Lord's, and He theirs.

Oh, that we could pour out our souls in prayer for the unconverted! You know where they will all be in a few years! Oh, by Your wrath, we pray, let them not endure it! By the flames of hell, be pleased to ransom them from going down into the pit! By everything that is dreadful in the wrath to come, we urge You to have mercy on these sons of men, even on those who have no mercy on themselves. Father, have You not promised Your Son to see His soul's travail? We point You to the ransom paid; we point You once again to the groans of

Your Son, to His agony and bloody sweat!
Turn, turn Your glorious eyes there. Look on
these sinners, speak the word, and bid them
live.

Righteous Father, refresh every corner of
the vineyard, and on every branch of the vine,
let the dew of heaven rest. Oh, that You would
bless Your church throughout the world! Let
visible union be established, or if not that, yet
let the invisible union that has always existed
be better recognized by believers. Will You repair our schisms? Will You repair the breaches
that have been made in the walls of Zion? Oh,
that You would purge us of everything un-
scriptural, until all Christians come to the law
and to the testimony and still keep the ordinances and the doctrines as they were committed to the apostles by Christ!

Remember our land in this time of need.
Be pleased by some means to relieve the
prevalent distress. Quicken the wheels of
commerce so that the many who are out of
employment may no longer be crying for work
and bread. Oh, that You would cause wars to
cease to the ends of the earth, or when they
break out, use them to break the slave's fet-
ters. Though desperate be the evil, yet grant
that Satan may cast out Satan, and may his
kingdom be divided and so fall.

Above all, long-expected Messiah, do come!
Your ancient people who despised You once
are waiting for You in Your second coming,

and we, the Gentiles, who did not know You or regard You, we, too, are watching for Your advent. Do not wait, O Jesus! May Your feet soon stand again on Mount Olivet! This time, You will not have to sweat great drops of blood there, but You will come to proclaim the year of vengeance for Your foes, and the year of acceptance for Your people.

> When wilt Thou the heavens rend,
> In majesty come down?

Earth travails for Your coming. The whole creation groans in pain together until now. Your own expect You. We are longing until we are weary for Your coming. Come quickly, Lord Jesus, come quickly.

5

To the King Eternal

Our God and Father, draw us to Yourself by Your Spirit, and may the few minutes that we spend in prayer be full of the true spirit of supplication. Grant that none of us with closed eyes may yet be looking abroad over the fields of vanity, but may our eyes be really shut to everything else but what is spiritual and divine. May we have communion with God in the secret places of our hearts and find Him to be a sanctuary.

O Lord, we do not find it easy to get rid of distracting thoughts, but we pray that You would help us to draw the sword against them and drive them away. As Abraham drove away the birds that came down upon his sacrifice (Genesis 15:11), so may we chase away all cares, all thoughts of pleasure, everything else, whether pleasing or painful, that would keep us away from real fellowship with the Father and with His Son, Jesus Christ.

We want to begin with adoration. We worship from our hearts the Three in One, the infinitely glorious Jehovah, the only living and true God. We adore the Father, the Son, and the Holy Spirit, the God of Abraham, of Isaac, and of Jacob. We have not yet ascended to the place where pure spirits behold the face of God, but we will soon be there, perhaps much sooner than we think. We desire to be there in spirit now, casting our crowns upon the glassy sea before the throne of the Infinite Majesty, and ascribing glory and honor, and power and praise, and dominion and might to Him who sits on the throne, and unto the Lamb forever and ever.

All the church worships You, O God. Every heart renewed by grace takes a delight in adoring You. We, among the rest, though least and lowest of them all, would yet bow as heartily as any, worshiping, loving, praising in our souls, being silent before God because our joy in Him is altogether inexpressible.

Lord, help us to worship You in life as well as by our lips. May our whole being be taken up with You. As the fire fell down on Elijah's sacrifice of old and licked up even the water that was in the trenches (1 Kings 18:30–39), so may the consuming fire of the divine Spirit use up all our nature. Even the thing that might seem to hinder, even out of that may God get glory by the removal of it. Thus would we adore You.

But, dear Savior, we come to You, and we remember what our state is. The condition we are in encourages us to come to You now as beggars, depending on Your heavenly charity. You are a Savior, and as such, You are looking for those who need saving, and here we are; here we come. We are the men and women You are looking for, needing a Savior.

Great Physician, we bring You our wounds and bruises and putrefying sores. The more diseased we are and the more conscious we are today of the depravity of our nature, of the deep-seated corruption of our hearts, the more we feel that we are the sort of beings that You are seeking, for the well and whole have no need of a physician, but those who are sick (Mark 2:17).

Glorious Benefactor, we can meet You on good terms, for we are full of poverty. We are just as empty as we can be. We could not be more abjectly dependent than we are. Since You want to display Your mercy, here is our sin. Since You want to show Your strength, here is our weakness. Since You want to manifest Your lovingkindness, here are our needs. Since You want to glorify Your grace, here we are, people who can never have a shadow of a hope except through Your grace, for we are undeserving, ill-deserving, hell-deserving. If You do not magnify Your grace in us, we must perish.

Somehow we feel that it is sweet to come to You in this way. If we had to tell You that we had some good thing in us that You required of us, we would have to question whether we were not flattering ourselves and presumptuously thinking that we were better than we are. Lord Jesus, we come just as we are. This is how we came at first, and this is how we come still—with all our failures, with all our transgressions, with all and everything that is what it ought not to be—we come to You. We do bless You that You receive us and our wounds, and by Your stripes we are healed (Isaiah 53:5). You receive us and our sins, and by Your sin-bearing we are set clear and free from sin. You receive us and our death, even our death, for You are He who lives, and was dead, and are alive forevermore (Revelation 1:18).

We simply come and lie at Your feet, obedient to that call of Yours, *"Come unto me, all ye that labour and are heavy laden, and I will give you rest"* (Matthew 11:28). Let us feel sweet rest, since we do come at Your call. May some come that have never come until this day, and may others who have been coming these many years consciously come again, coming unto You *"as unto a living stone...chosen of God, and precious"* (1 Peter 2:4), to build our everlasting hopes upon.

But, Lord, now that we have come so near to You and are on right terms with You, we venture to ask You this, that we who love You may love You much, much more. Oh, since You have been precious, Your very name has music in it to our ears, and there are times when Your love is so inexpressibly strong upon us that we are carried away with it. We have felt that we would gladly die to increase Your honor. We have been willing to lose our name and our reputation if You might be glorified through that. Truly, we often feel that if the crushing of us would lift You one inch higher, we would gladly suffer it.

For You, blessed King, we would set the crown on Your head, even if the sword would smite our arm off at the shoulder blade. You must be King, You must be glorified, no matter what becomes of us.

Yet we have to mourn because we do not always feel this rapture and ardor of love as we should. Oh, at times You manifest Yourself to us so charmingly that heaven itself could scarcely be happier than our world becomes when You are with us in it. But when You are gone and we are in the dark, give us the love that loves in the dark, that loves when there is no comforting sense of Your presence. Do not let us depend on feelings; may we always love You. If You were to turn Your back on us for a whole year, may we still think no less of You, for You are to be unspeakably loved whatever You do. If You give us rough words, may we still cling to You. And if the rod is used until we tingle, may we still love You, for You are to be infinitely loved by all men and angels. As Your Father loves You, make our hearts love

You always the same. With all the capacity for love that there is in us, and with all the more that You can give us, may we love our Lord in spirit and in truth.

Help us, Lord, to conquer sin out of love for You. Help some dear strugglers who have been mastered by sin sometimes, but who are struggling against it. Give them the victory, Lord. When the battle gets very sharp and they are tempted to give way a little, help them to be very firm and very strong, never giving up hope in the Lord Jesus, and resolving that if they perish, they will perish at His feet and nowhere else but there.

Lord, raise up in our churches many men and women who are all on fire with love for Christ and His divine Gospel. Oh, give us again men like Antipas, Your faithful martyr, and men like Paul, Your earnest servant who proclaimed Your truth so boldly. Give us Johns, men to whom the Spirit speaks, who will have us hear what the Spirit says to the churches. Lord, revive us! Revive Your work in the midst of the years in all the churches. Return to the church of God in this country. Return to her. Your adversaries think that they will have it all their own way, but they will not, for the Lord lives, and blessed be our Rock (Psalm 18:46).

Because of truth and righteousness, we implore You, lay bare Your arm in these last days. O Shepherd of Israel, deal a heavy blow at the wolves, and keep Your sheep in their own true pastures, free from the poisonous pastures of error. O God, we want to stir You up. We know You do not sleep, and yet sometimes it seems as if You nap awhile and allow things to go on in their own way.

We entreat You, awake. Plead Your own cause. We know Your answer: *"Awake, awake; put on thy strength, O Zion"* (Isaiah 52:1). This we want to do, Lord, but we cannot do it unless You put forth Your strength to turn our weakness into might.

Great God, save this nation! O God of heaven and earth, stop the floods of infidelity and filthiness that roll over this land. O God, may we see better days! Men seem entirely indifferent now. They will not come to hear the Word as they once did. God of our fathers, let Your Spirit work again among the masses. Turn the hearts of the people to the hearing of the Word, and convert them when they hear it. May it be preached with the Holy Spirit sent down from heaven.

Our hearts are weary for You, O King, You King forgotten in Your own land, You King despised among Your own people. When will You yet be glorious before the eyes of all mankind? Come, we implore You, come quickly (Revelation 22:20), or if You do not come personally, send forth the Holy Spirit with a greater power than ever so that our hearts may leap within us as they see miracles of mercy repeated in our midst.

Father, glorify Your Son. Somehow our prayer always comes to this before we finish. *"Father...glorify thy Son, that thy Son also may glorify thee"* (John 17:1). Let the days come when He will see the travail of His soul and will be satisfied (Isaiah 53:11). Bless all work done for You, whether it is in the barn or in the cathedral, silently and quietly in the street, or in the Sunday school or in the classroom. O Lord, bless Your work. Hear also prayers that have been offered up by wives for their husbands, children for their parents, parents for their children. Let the holy service of prayer never cease, and let the intercession be accepted by God, for Jesus Christ's sake.

6

The Wonders of Calvary

reat God Almighty, there was a time when we dreaded the thought of coming near to You, for we were guilty, and You were angry with us. But now we will praise You because Your anger is turned away, and You comfort us. Now the very throne that was once a place of dread has now become the place of shelter. We flee to You to hide us.

We long to get away from the world, even from the remembrance of it, and have fellowship with the world to come by speaking with Him who *"was, and is, and is to come"* (Revelation 4:8), the Almighty. Lord, we have often been worried and wearied with care, but with You, care comes to an end. All things are with You, and when we live in You, we live in wealth, in sure repose, in constant joy.

We battle with the sons of men against a thousand errors and unrighteousnesses, but when we flee to You, all is truth and purity and holiness, and our hearts find peace. Above all, we have to battle with ourselves, and we are very much ashamed of ourselves. After many years of great mercy, after tasting the powers of the world to come, we still are so weak, so foolish. But when we get away from self to God, there we find truth and purity and holiness, and our hearts rest in peace, wisdom, completeness, delight, joy, and victory.

Oh, bring us now, we pray, near to Yourself. Let us bathe ourselves in communion with our God. Blessed be the love that chose us before the world began. We can never sufficiently adore You for Your sovereignty, the sovereignty of love that saw us in the ruins of the Fall, yet loved us notwithstanding all.

We praise the God of the eternal council chamber and the everlasting covenant. Yet we struggle to find sufficiently worthy words with which to praise Him who gave us grace in Christ His Son, before He spread the starry sky.

We also bless You, O God, as the God of our redemption, for You have loved us so much that You even gave Your dear Son for us. He gave Himself, His very life for us, so that He might redeem us from all iniquity and sanctify us for Himself to be His special people, zealous for good works (Titus 2:14).

We can never sufficiently adore free grace and dying love. The wonders of Calvary never cease to be wonders. They grow marvelous in our eyes as we think of Him who washed us from our sins in His own blood. Nor can we cease to praise the God of our regeneration, who found us dead and made us live, found us at enmity and reconciled us, found us loving the things of this world and lifted us out of the morass and mire of selfishness and worldliness into the love of divine, everlasting things.

O Spirit of God, we love You this day, especially for dwelling in us. How can You abide in so crude a habitation? How can You make these bodies Your temples? And yet You did so. For that, let Your name be held in reverence as long as we live.

O Lord, we want to delight ourselves in You this day. Give us faith and love and hope so that, with these three graces, we may draw very near to the triune God. You will keep us, You will preserve us, You will feed us, You will lead us, and You will bring us to the mind of God. There You will show us Your love, and in the glory everlasting and boundless, there You will make us know and taste and feel the joys that cannot be expressed.

But a little longer waiting and we will come to the golden shore. But a little longer fighting and we will receive the crown of life that does not fade away.

Lord, get us up above the world. Come, Holy Spirit, heavenly Dove, mount and bear us on Your wings, far from these inferior sorrows and inferior joys, up where eternal ages roll. May we ascend in joyful contemplation, and may our spirits come back again, strong for all service, armed for all battles, armored for all dangers, and made ready to live heaven on earth, until by and by we will live heaven in heaven. Great Father, be with Your waiting people. Any in great trouble, may You greatly help. Any who are despondent, may You sweetly comfort and cheer. Any who have erred and are suffering under their own sin, may You bring them back and heal their wounds. Any who this day are panting after holiness, may You give them the desire of their hearts. Any who are longing for usefulness, may You lead them into ways of usefulness.

Lord, we want to live while we live. We do pray that we may not merely groan out an existence here below, or live as earthworms crawling back into our holes and dragging now and then a dry leaf with us. Rather, give us the ability to live as we ought to live, with a new life that You have put into us, with the divine awakening that has lifted us as much above common men as men are lifted above the beasts that perish.

Do not let us always be hampered like poor half-hatched birds within the eggshell. May we chip the shell today and get out into the glorious liberty of the children of God. Grant us this, we pray.

Lord, visit our churches. We have heard Your message to the churches at Ephesus; it is a message to us also. Do not let any of us lose our first love. Do not let our churches grow cold and dead. We are not, we fear, what we once were. Lord, revive us! All our help must come from You. Give back to the church its love, its confidence, its holy daring, its consecration, its liberality, its holiness. Give back all that it ever had, and give it much more. Take every member and wash his feet most tenderly. Sweet Lord, set us with clean feet in a clean road, with clean hearts to guide us. May You bless us, as You are disposed to do, in a divine way.

Bless us, our Father, and let all the churches of Jesus Christ partake of the same care and tenderness. Walking among the golden candlesticks, Lord, trim every lamp and make every light, even though it burns but feebly now, to shine out gloriously through Your care.

Now bless the sinners. Lord, convert them. O God, save men. Save this great city, this wicked city, this slumbering, dead city. Lord, arouse it, arouse it by any means, so that it may turn to its God. Lord, save sinners all the world over.

Let Your precious Word be fulfilled: *"Behold, he cometh with clouds"* (Revelation 1:7). Why do You wait? Do not wait, O Lord. And now unto the Father, Son, and Holy Spirit be glory forever and ever.

7

"Let All the People Praise Thee"

ur Father, when we read Your description of human nature, we are sure it is true, for You have seen man ever since his fall, and You have been grieved at heart concerning him. Moreover, You have such a love toward him that You did not judge him harshly. Every word that You have spoken must be according to truth. You have measured and computed the iniquity of man, for You have laid it on the Well Beloved, and we know You have not laid on Him more than is just.

O God, we are distressed and greatly bowed down when we see the condition to which we and all our race have fallen. *"Where is boasting then?"* (Romans 3:27). And yet we grieve to say that we do boast, have boasted, and that our fellowmen are great at boasting. Instead, we ought to lay our hands upon our mouths before You.

It is a wonder to us that You should look upon man at all. The most hateful object in creation must be a man, because he killed Your Son, because he has multiplied rebellions against Your holy law. Yet truly there is no sight that gives You more pleasure than man, for Jesus became a man. The brightness of His glory covers all our shame, and the pureness and perfection of His obedience shines like the sun in the midst of the darkness. For His sake, You are well pleased, and You dwell with us.

Lord, we once thought that those descriptions of our hearts were somewhat exaggerated, but we do not think so now. Truly we perceive that had it not been for restraint that held us like chains, we, in our unregenerate state, were capable of anything. Even now, when we are regenerate, the old sin that remains in us is capable of reaching a high degree of infamy. If the new life did not restrain the old death, we do not know what we might yet become.

We once thought we were humble, but we soon found that our pride will feed on any current flattery that is laid at our door. We thought we were believers, but sometimes we are so doubting, so unbelieving, so vexed with skepticism, that we would not certainly choose to follow. That is Your work in us. By nature we are such liars that we think You are a liar, too—the surest token of our untruthfulness is that we think that You could be untrue.

Oh, these wicked hearts of ours! Do they not have enough kindling in them to set on fire the course of nature? If only a spark were to fall into them, any one of our members left to itself would dishonor Christ, deny the Lord who bought us, and turn back into perdition.

We are altogether ashamed. Truly in us is fulfilled Your own Word: *"That thou...never open thy mouth any more because of thy shame"* (Ezekiel 16:63). Your love to us has silenced us. That great love has hidden boasting away from us—Your great love, with which You loved us even when we *"were dead in trespasses and sins"* (Ephesians 2:1); Your great love with which You have loved us still, despite our poor manners, our wanderings, our shortcomings, and our excesses.

Oh, the matchless love of God! Truly if there is any glory, it must all be the Lord's. If there is any virtue, it is the result of grace. If there is anything whatsoever that lifts us above the Devil himself, it is the work of the divine Spirit, to whom be glory!

At the remembrance of all this, and being in Your presence, we rejoice that our unrighteousness is covered, that we are free from condemnation, and that we are the favored of the Lord. You have allowed us, O Lord, to taste of the love that is not merely laid up for us, for we have enjoyed it and do enjoy it still.

Our hearts know the Father's love, for we *"have received the Spirit of adoption, whereby we cry, Abba, Father"* (Romans 8:15). We joy and rejoice in the redemption of our spirits, and we expect the redemption of our bodies, when at the coming of the Lord, they, too, *"shall be raised incorruptible, and we shall be changed"* (1 Corinthians 15:52).

O Jesus, You will bring Israel out of Egypt, and not a hoof will be left behind—no, not a bone or any piece of Your elect will be left in the hands of the Adversary. We will come out clean, delivered by Him who does nothing by halves, but who on the cross said, *"It is finished"* (John 19:30), and who much more will say it on His throne. Glory be unto the Father, Son, and Holy Spirit, who lifted us up from our ruin and condemnation, made us new creatures, justified us, and guaranteed us eternal life that will be manifested at the coming of the Lord. All glory be unto His blessed name forever and ever!

Now, Lord, during the few days that remain to us here below, let it be all our business to cry, *"Behold the Lamb"* (John 1:29)! Oh, teach these hearts to be always conscious of Your love; and then teach these lips that they may express as best they can with Your divine help the matchless story of the Cross. Oh, give us the privilege of winning many to Jesus. Do not let us be barren, but may we be able to cry that we are the beloved of the Lord, and all our offspring are with us. May we have many spiritual offspring who will go with us to the throne, so that we may say before Him, *"I and the children whom the* LORD *hath given me"* (Isaiah 8:18).

Lord, bless the work of the churches and all their branches. Let Your kingdom come into the hearts of multitudes through the churches. Remember all churches that are really at work for Jesus, and all private individuals, workers alone, workers by themselves. Let the Lord's own name be made known by tens of thousands. Give the Word, and may the company of those who publish it be great. Let our beloved country know Christ and come to His feet. Let the dark places of our cities be enlightened with the sweet name of Jesus. And then let the heathen know You, and the ends of the earth hear of You.

Oh, from the tree declare Your salvation, and from the throne let it be published in the proclamations of a king. *"Let the people praise thee, O God; let all the people praise thee"* (Psalm 67:3).

Our hearts seem as if they have nothing else to ask for when they reach this point. Yet we want to go back a moment and say, "Lord, forgive our sins; Lord, sanctify our persons; Lord, guide us in difficulty; Lord, supply our needs. May He teach us, perfect us, comfort us, and prepare us for the appearing of His Son from heaven!"

And now we come back to a theme that still seems to engross our desires. Oh, that Christ would come! Oh, that His Word would be made known to the ends of the earth! Lord, they die, they perish, they pass away by multitudes! Every time the sun rises and sets, they pass away! Do not wait, we entreat You. Give wings to the feet of Your messengers and fire to their mouths, so that they may proclaim the Word with Pentecostal swiftness and might. Oh, that Your kingdom would come, and Your will be done on earth as it is in heaven, *"for thine is the kingdom, and the power, and the glory, for ever. Amen"* (Matthew 6:13).

8

A Prayer for Holiness

Our Father, we worship and love You. It is one point of our worship that You are holy. There was a time when we loved You for Your mercy, for we knew no more. But now You have changed our hearts and made us in love with goodness, purity, justice, true holiness. We understand now why the cherubim and seraphim continually cry, *"Holy, holy, holy, Lord God Almighty"* (Revelation 4:8).

We adore You because You are holy, and we love You for Your infinite perfection. Now we sigh and cry after holiness ourselves. Sanctify us wholly, spirit, soul, and body. Lord, we mourn over the sins of our pasts and our present shortcomings. We bless You, for You have forgiven us. We are reconciled to You by the death of Your Son. There are many who know that they have been washed, and that He who bears away sin has borne their sin away.

51

These are they who cry to You to be delivered from the power of sin, to be delivered from the power of temptation without, but especially from indwelling sin within.

Lord, purify us in head, heart, and hand. If it is necessary that we should be put into the fire to be refined as silver is refined, we would even welcome the fire, if we may be rid of the dross. Lord, save us from constitutional sin, from sins of temperament, from sins of our surroundings. Save us from ourselves in every shape, and grant us especially to have the light of love strong within us.

May we love You, God. May we love You, O Savior. May we love the people of God as being members of one body in connection with You. May we love the guilty world with the love that desires its salvation and conversion. May we love not in word only, but in deed and in truth (1 John 3:18). May we help the helpless, comfort the mourner, sympathize with the widow and fatherless, and may we always be ready to put up with wrong, to be long-suffering, to be very patient, full of forgiveness, counting it a small thing that we should forgive our fellow-men since we have been forgiven by God. Lord, tune our hearts to love, and then give us an inward peace, a restfulness about everything.

May we have no burden to carry because, though we have a burden, we have rolled it upon the Lord. May we take up our cross, and because Christ has once died on the cross, may our cross become a comfort to us. May we count it all joy when we fall into various trials, knowing that in all this God will be glorified, His image will be stamped on us, and the eternal purpose will be fulfilled, in which He has predestined us *"to be conformed to the image of his Son"* (Romans 8:29).

Lord, look upon Your people. We could pray about our troubles, but we will not do so right now. We will only pray against our sins. We could come to You about our weariness, about our sickness, about our disappointment, about our poverty, but we will leave all that for now. We will only come about sin. Lord, make us holy, and then do what You will with us.

We ask You, O Lord, help us to adorn the doctrine of God our Savior in all things. If we are fighting against sin—*"the sin which doth so easily beset us"* (Hebrews 12:1)—Lord, lend us heavenly weapons and heavenly strength so that we may cut the giants down, these men of Anak that come against us (Numbers 13:33). We feel very feeble. Oh, make us *"strong in the Lord, and in the power of his might"* (Ephesians 6:10). May we never let sin have any rest in us. May we chase it, drive it out, slay it, hang it on a tree, abhor it, and may we ever *"cleave to that which is good"* (Romans 12:9).

Some of us are trying, striving after some excellent virtue. Lord, help strugglers. Enable those who contend against great difficulties to see greater grace, have more faith, and be nearer to God. Lord, we will be holy, and by Your grace we will never rest until we are. You have begun a good work in us, and You will carry it on (Philippians 1:6). You will work in us to will and to do of Your own good pleasure (Philippians 2:13).

Lord, help the converted child to be correct in his relationship to his parents. Help the Christian father and mother to be right in dealing with their children. May they not *"provoke...*[their] *children to anger, lest they be discouraged"* (Colossians 3:21). Take away willfulness from the young. Take away impatience from the old. Lord, help Christian men of business to act uprightly. May Christian masters never be harsh with their servants, with their workers. May Christian workers give to their masters what is just and equal in the way of work in return for wages. May we as Christians always stand on our rights, but also be willing to minister to the needs of others.

Oh, that as Christians we might be humble! Lord, take away that stiff-necked, proud look. Take away from us the spirit of "stand away, for I am holier than thou." Make us reach out to men of low social standing, yes, and even to men of low morals, low character. May we seek them out, seek their good. Oh, give to the church of Christ an intense love for the souls of men. May it make our hearts break to think that they will perish in their sin. May we grieve every day because of the sin of our cities. Put a mark on our foreheads, and let us be known to You as men who sigh and cry for all the abominations that are done in the midst of our cities (Ezekiel 9:4).

O God, save us from a hard heart, an unkind spirit, that is insensible to the woes of others. Lord, preserve Your people also from worldliness, from rioting, from drunkenness, from clamoring and lewdness, from strife and envy, from everything that would dishonor the name of Christ that we bear. Lord, make us holy. Our prayer comes back to this: make us holy. Cleanse the inside and let the outside be clean, too. Make us holy, O God. Do this for Christ's sake. It is not that we hope to be saved by our own holiness, but holiness is salvation. When we are holy, we are saved from sin.

Lord, help Your poor children to be holy. Oh, keep us so if we are so. Keep us even from stumbling, and present us faultless before Your presence at last (Jude 24).

We pray for friends who are ill, for many who are troubled because of the illness of others. We bring before You every case of trouble and trial known to us and ask for Your gracious intervention. We pray for Your ministers everywhere. For Your missionary servants, we ask You to remember those who are making great sacrifice out in the hot sun or in the cold and frozen North. Everywhere preserve those who for Christ's sake carry their lives in their hands.

Our brothers and sisters, in poverty many of them, working for Christ, Lord accept them and help us to help them. Do remember the Sunday school teachers, the city missionaries, along with those who visit and hand out tracts door-to-door, and all who in any way endeavor to bring Christ to the notice of men. Oh, help them all.

We will offer but one more prayer, and it is this. Lord, look in pity on any who are not in Christ. May they be converted. May they pass from death to life and never forget it. May they see the eternal light for the first time, and may they remember it even in eternity. Father, help us. Bless us now for Jesus' sake.

9

Glorious Liberty

Our Father, we bless Your name that we can say from the bottom of our hearts, *"Abba, Father"* (Romans 8:15). It is the chief joy of our lives that we have become the children of God by faith that is in Christ Jesus, and we can in the deep calm of our spirits say, *"Our Father which art in heaven, Hallowed be thy name. Thy kingdom come. Thy will be done in earth, as it is in heaven"* (Matthew 6:9–10).

Lord, we thank You for the liberty that comes to our emancipated spirits through the adoption that You have made us to enjoy. When we were in servitude, the chains were heavy, for we could not keep Your law. There was an inward spirit of rebellion. When the commandment came, it irritated our corrupt nature, sin revived, and we died.

Even in the moments when we had some inner striving for better things, the power that was in us lusted to evil, and the spirit of Hagar's Ishmael was upon us. We wanted to get away from the Father's house. We were wild men, men of the wilderness, and we did not love living in the Father's house.

O God, we thank You that we have not been cast out. Indeed, if You had cast out the child of the bondwoman, You would have cast us all out, but now through sovereign grace all is altered with us. Blessed be Your name. It is a work of divine power and love over human nature, for now we are the children of the promise, certainly not born according to the strength of the human will, or of blood, or of birth, but born by the Holy Spirit through the power of the Word, *"begotten...again unto a lively hope by the resurrection of Jesus Christ from the dead"* (1 Peter 1:3), children of the Great Father who is in heaven, having His life within us. Now, like Isaac, we are heirs according to promise and heirs of the promise. We dwell at home in the Father's house, and our souls are satisfied as with marrow and fatness, and our mouths will praise You as with joyful lips (Psalm 63:5).

O God, we would not trade places with angels, much less with kings of the earth. To be indeed Your sons and daughters—the thought of it brings to our souls a present heaven, and the fruition of it will be our heaven, to dwell forever in the house of the Lord, and leave it no more, but to be His sons and His heirs forever.

Our prayer is for others who are still in bondage. We thank You, Lord, that You have given them the spirit of bondage and made them to fear. We are glad that they are brought to feel the evil of sin, to feel the perfection of Your law, to know something of the fiery nature of Your justice, and so to be shut up unto salvation by grace through faith. But, Lord, do not let them remain long under the harsh teacher, but may the schoolmaster with his rod bring them to Christ. (See Galatians 3:24.)

Lord, cure any of Your chosen of self-righteousness. Deliver them from any hope in their own abilities, but keep them low. Bring them out of any hope of salvation by their own prayers or their own repentance. Bring them to cast themselves upon Your grace to be saved by trusting in Christ. Emancipate them from all observance of days, weeks, months, years, and things of human institution. Bring them into the glorious liberty of the children of God so that Your law may become their delight, so that You may become their strength and their all, and so that Your Son may become their joy and their crown. We do pray this with all our hearts.

Lord, deliver any of Your children from quarreling with You. Help us to be always at one with our God. *"It is the LORD: let him do what seemeth him good"* (1 Samuel 3:18), and blessed be His name forever and ever.

God bless our country, and the sister country across the ocean, and all lands where Your name is known and reverenced, and heathen lands where it is unknown. Everywhere may the Lord's kingdom come and His name be glorified. Glory be to the Father, and to the Son, and to the Holy Spirit, as it was in the beginning, is now, and ever will be, world without end.

10

The Music of Praise

 blessed God, we must be helped by Your Spirit or we cannot worship You fittingly. Behold, the holy angels adore You, and the hosts redeemed by blood bring everlasting hallelujahs to Your feet. What are we, the creatures of a day, polluted with sin, that we should think that we can praise You? And yet the music of praise would not be complete if Your children did not join in it, even those of them who are still in this world below. Help us, then. Enable us to tune our harps and to bring forth music from our spirits.

Truly, Lord, if there are any creatures in the world that can praise You, we ought to do so. Each one among us feels that he has some special reason for gratitude. Lord, it is an unspeakable mercy to know You—to know You as our reconciled God, to know You as our Father in Christ Jesus, who has forgiven us all our trespasses. Oh, it is unspeakably sweet to come and rest in You, and to know that there is now no cause of quarrel between us and You. On the contrary, we realize that we are bound to one another by a covenant that in infinite tenderness and mercy You have made, so that Your people might have strong consolation and might boldly take hold of You.

Oh, the joy of knowing that we are Yours forever, Yours in the trials of life, and Yours in the last dread trial of death, and then Yours in resurrection, Yours throughout eternity! We do therefore worship You, O God, not under coercion, nor under terror or pressure, but cheerfully and gladly, ascribing unto You praise, power, dominion, glory, and honor, world without end.

We wish we knew how to do something for You. We pray that we may be helped to do so before we die. May every fleeting hour confess that we have brought Your Gospel some renown. May we so live as to extend the Redeemer's kingdom at least in some little measure. May ours not be fruitless, wasted lives. May no faculty of ours lay by and rust, but to the utmost of our capacity, may we be helped by the divine Spirit to spend the whole of our lives in real adoration.

We know that he who serves is actually praying, he who gives is actually praising, and he who obeys is actually adoring. The life is the best music. Oh, set it to good music, we pray, and help us throughout all our lives to keep to the right notes. May there be no false pitch in all the singing of our lives, but let all be according to that sacred score that is written out so fully in the life music of our Lord.

We implore You to look down upon Your children and cheer us. Lord, lift us up. Come, Holy Spirit, like a fresh, invigorating wind. Let our spirits, through Your Spirit, rise upward toward God.

With much shamefacedness we acknowledge our transgressions and sins. However, there are some who have never felt the burden of sin at all. Lord, lay it on them; press them with it. Almighty God, vex their souls. Let them find no rest until they find rest in You. May they never be content to live and die in sin, but in Your infinite mercy, come to them and make them sorry for their sin.

As for Your people, we are grieved to think that we do not live better than we do. Blessed be Your name for every fruit of holiness, for every work of faith, but oh, for more. You have changed the tree; it is no longer a bramble. It can bring forth figs, but now we want to bring forth more of these sweet fruits.

Lord, make us to love Christ intensely, to love the souls of men most heartily, to love Your truth with earnestness, to love the name of Jesus above everything. May we be ravished with the sound of it. May the Lord give us every grace, not only love, but faith, hope, holy gentleness, meekness, patience, and brotherly love. Build us up, we pray, Lord, in all knowledge and in all experience. Give us, along with submission to Your will, holy resignation, great watchfulness, much carefulness in our speech, so that we may rule the tongue and so rule the whole body.

Lord, may You pour out Your Spirit upon us so that every chamber of our nature may be sweetened and perfumed with the indwelling of God, until our imaginations only delight in things chaste and pure; until our memories cast out the vile stuff from the dark chambers; until we expect and long for heavenly things; until our treasure all is in heaven, and our hearts are there. Take our highest manhood, Lord, and saturate it in Your love, until, like Gideon's fleece, it is filled with dew, every lock and every single fleck of it, not a single portion of it left unmoistened by the dew from heaven.

How we bless You, Lord, for many who are striving to walk as Christ walked, and who are also trying to bring others to Christ. O Lord, help us in this struggle after holiness and usefulness. As You have given to many the desire of their hearts in this respect up to a certain measure, now enlarge their hearts, and give them more both of holiness and usefulness. May we be like trees *"planted by the rivers of water"* (Psalm 1:3), so that we ourselves may be vigorous. Give us the ability to bring forth abundant fruit according to our season

(Psalm 1:3), to the everlasting praise and glory of God.

Our desire is that we may be quickened in our progress toward the celestial life. Visit us with Your salvation. Lord, let us not only have life, but let us have it more abundantly (John 10:10). May we every one of us quicken his pace, and may we run more earnestly than ever toward the mark that is set before us.

Remember all Your church throughout the whole world. Prosper missionary operations. Be with any ministers or missionaries who are depressed for lack of success. Be with any who are rejoicing because of success. May each heart be kept in a right state, so that You may use Your servants to the utmost possibility.

O God, send us better days than these, we pray. We thank You for all the light there is, but send us more light. We thank You for what life there is among Christians, but send more of it.

Bind the churches together in unity, and then give them such speed, such force, such power, that they will break into the ranks of the Adversary and the victory be unto Christ and to His people.

Remember our dear country. Bless the head of our nation. Remember all those who lead our legislature. Be gracious to all ranks and conditions of men. Have mercy on all who are poor and needy, on all who are sick and sorrowing, and who are tossed upon the sea.

Remember the prisoners and those who have no helper. Be gracious to those who are in the summons of death. Finally, let the day come when the Son will shine forth in all His brightness, even Christ Jesus will be manifested, to be admired in them who believe and to make glad the whole creation. Do not wait, O Son of Righteousness, but come forth speedily. We ask it for Your name's sake.

11

Under the Blood

ehovah, our God, we thank You for leaving on record the story of Your ancient people. It is full of instruction to us. Help us to take its warning to avoid the faults into which they fell! You are a covenant God, and You keep Your promises. Your Word never fails. We have proved this to be so:

> Thus far we find that promise good,
> Which Jesus ratified with blood.

Nonetheless, as for ourselves, we are like Israel of old, a fickle people. We confess with great shame that although there are days when we take the tambourine and sing with Miriam *"unto the LORD, for he hath triumphed gloriously"* (Exodus 15:1), yet, not many hours later, we are thirsty, we cry for water, and we murmur in our tents. Bitter Marah turns our hearts (vv. 22–25), and we are grieved with You, our God. When we behold Your Sinai covered in smoke, we bow before You with reverence and awe, but there have been times when we have set up the golden calf and have said of some earthly things, *"These be thy gods, O Israel"* (Exodus 32:4). We believe with intensity of faith and then doubt with a horribleness of doubt.

Lord, You have been very patient with us. Many have been our provocations, many have been Your chastisements, but

> Your strokes are fewer than our crimes,
>   And lighter than our guilt.

You *"hath not dealt with us after our sins; nor rewarded us according to our iniquities"* (Psalm 103:10). Blessed be Your name!

And now fulfill that part of the covenant wherein You have said, *"A new heart also will I give you, and a new spirit will I put within you"* (Ezekiel 36:26). *"I will put my fear in their hearts, that they shall not depart from me"* (Jeremiah 32:40). Hold us fast, and then we will hold fast to You. Turn us, and we will be turned. Keep us, and we will keep Your statutes.

We cry to You that we may no longer provoke You. We beg You to send the serpents among us rather than to let sin come among us. Oh, that we might have our eyes always on the bronze serpent that heals all the bites of evil (Numbers 21:9), but may we not look to sin or love it. Do not let the devices of Balaam and of Balak prevail against us, to lead Your people away from their purity. Do not let us be defiled with false doctrine or with unholy living, but may we walk as the separated people of God and keep ourselves unspotted from the world. Lord, we do not want to grieve Your Spirit. May we never vex You so as to lead You in Your wrath to say, *"They shall not enter into my rest"* (Hebrews 3:11). Bear with us still for the dear sake of Him whose blood is upon us. Bear with us still. Do not send the destroying angel as You did to Egypt, but again fulfill that promise of Yours: *"When I see the blood, I will pass over you"* (Exodus 12:13).

Just now may we be consciously passed over by the Spirit of condemnation. May we know in our hearts that *"there is therefore now no condemnation to them which are in Christ Jesus"* (Romans 8:1). May we feel the peace-giving power of divine absolution. May we come into Your holy presence with our feet washed in the bronze laver, hearing our Great High Priest say to us, "[You are] *clean every whit"* (John 13:10). Thus made clean, may we draw near to God through Jesus Christ our Lord.

Further, our heavenly Father, we come before You now washed in the blood, wearing the snowy-white robe of Christ's righteousness, and we ask You to remember Your people. Some are sorely burdened. Lighten the burden or strengthen the shoulder. Some are bowed down with fear, and perhaps they mistrust You. Forgive the mistrust, and give a great increase of faith so that they may trust You where they cannot trace You. Lord, remember any who bear the burdens of others. Some cry to You day and night about the sins of the times, about the wanderings of Your church. Lord, hear our prayers! We want to bear this yoke for You, but help us to bear it without the fear that causes us to distrust You. May we know that You will take care of Your own case and preserve Your own truth, and may we thus be restful about it all.

Some are crying to You for the conversion of relatives and friends. They have taken up this burden to follow after Jesus in the matter of cross bearing. Grant them to see the desire of their hearts fulfilled. God, save our children and our children's children, and if we have unconverted relatives of any kind, Lord, have mercy on them for Christ's sake. Give us joy in them—as much joy in them as Christians as we have had sorrow about them as unbelievers.

Further, be pleased to visit Your church with the Holy Spirit. Renew the Day of Pentecost in our midst. In the midst of all gatherings of Your people, may there come the descension of the holy fire, the uprising of the heavenly wind. May matters that are now slow and dead become quick and full of life, and may the Lord

Jesus Christ be exalted in the midst of His church, which is His fullness, *"the fulness of him that filleth all in all"* (Ephesians 1:23). May multitudes be converted. May they come flocking to Christ with holy eagerness to find in Him a refuge, even as the doves fly to their dovecotes.

Oh, for salvation work throughout these islands, across the sea, and in every part of the world, especially in heathen lands. Bring many to Christ's feet, we pray, everywhere that men are ready to lay down their lives to impart the heavenly life of Christ. Lord, work mightily! Your church cries to You, "Do not leave us. We can do nothing without You!" Our strength is wholly Yours. Come to us with great power, and let Your Word have free course and be glorified.

Remember everyone who calls You Father. May Your Father's love look on all the children. May the special need of each one be supplied, the special sorrow of each one be eased. May we be growing Christians; may we be working Christians; may we be perfected Christians; may we come to *"the measure of the stature of the fulness of Christ"* (Ephesians 4:13). Lord Jesus, You are a great pillar. In You all fullness dwells (Colossians 1:19). You began Your ministry with filling the waterpots full. You filled Simon Peter's boat until it began to sink. You filled the house where Your people met together with the presence of the Holy Spirit. You fill heaven. You will surely fill all things. Fill us; oh, fill us today with all the fullness of God! Thus make Your people joyful, strong, gracious, and heavenly!

But we cannot end our prayer when we have prayed for just Your people, though we have asked large things. We want You to look among the thousands and millions all around us who do not know You. Lord, look on the masses who go nowhere to worship. Have pity on them. *"Father, forgive them; for they know not what they do"* (Luke 23:34). Give them a desire to hear Your Word. Send the people a desire for their God.

O Lord, take sinners in hand Yourself. Come and reach obstinate, hardened minds. Let the careless and the frivolous begin to think about eternal things. May there be an uneasiness of heart, a sticking of the arrows of God in their bodies. May they seek the Great Physician and find healing this very day. Lord, You say, *"To day if ye will hear* [My] *voice, harden not your heart"* (Psalm 95:7–8), and we take up the echo. Save men today, even today. Bring them Your Spirit in power so that they may be willing to rest in Christ. Lord, hear, forgive, accept, and bless for Jesus' sake. Amen.

12

On Holy Ground

"*Our Father which art in heaven, Hallowed be thy name. Thy kingdom come. Thy will be done in earth, as it is in heaven*" (Matthew 6:9–10). I fear that we often begin our prayers with petitions for ourselves, putting our daily bread before Your kingdom and the pardoning of our sins before the hallowing of Your name. We do not want to do so today, but guided by our Lord's model of prayer, we want to first pray for Your glory. Here, great God, we want to adore You. You have made us and not we ourselves; we are Your people, and the sheep of Your pasture (Psalm 100:3). All glory be unto You, Jehovah, the only living and true God.

With heart and mind, memory and fear, hope and joy, we worship the Most High. It well becomes us to take our shoes off when we draw near to God, for the place where we stand is holy ground. If God in the bush demanded the unsandaled foot of the prophet (Exodus 3:4–5), how much more will God in Christ Jesus?

With the lowliest reverence, with the truest love, we worship God in Christ Jesus, uniting in this act with all the redeemed host above, with angels and principalities and powers. We cannot cast crowns at Your feet, for we do not have any yet, but if there is any virtue, if there is any praise, if there is about us anything of grace and good report, we ascribe it all to God. We cannot veil our faces with our wings, for we have none, but we veil them with something better than angelic wings: the blood and righteousness of Jesus Christ. With these we cover our faces, with these we cover our feet, and with these we fly up to God in holiest fellowship. *"Blessing, and honour, and glory, and power, be unto him that sitteth upon the throne, and unto the Lamb for ever and ever"* (Revelation 5:13).

Great God, we long that You may be known to the ends of the earth, that the idols may be utterly abolished. We long that false doctrine may fly like birds of darkness before the light and Your coming. Reign in the hearts of our fellowmen, Lord; subdue sin, and under Your feet let drunkenness, unchastity, oppression, and every form of wickedness be put away by the Gospel of Jesus Christ and His Holy Spirit.

Oh, that today, even today, many hearts might be won to God! Convince men of the wrong of being alienated from God, put into their hearts sorrow for sin and dread of the wrath to come, and lead and drive men to Christ. Oh, how we pray for the salvation of our fellowmen, not so much for their sakes as for the sake of the glory of God and the rewarding of Christ for His pain.

With all our hearts we pray, *"Thy kingdom come. Thy will be done in earth, as it is in heaven"* (Matthew 6:10). Lord, help us to do Your will. Take the crippled kingdom of our personhood and reign over it. Let spirit and body be consecrated to God. May there be no reserves. May everything be given up to You. Reign forever! Pierced King, despised and nailed to a tree, sit on the glorious, high throne in our hearts. May our lives prove that You are Lord over us by our every thought, desire, imagination, word, and act, in every respect being under Your divine control.

Out of their very hearts, Your people breathe to You the prayer that You may reign over us without a rival. O Savior, use for Yourself what You have bought with blood, and drive out the enemy. Let no power have any dominion over us except the power of Your good Spirit, who works righteousness and peace.

We pray today also that Your truth may prevail against the many antichrists that have gone forth against it. Our Father, restore a pure language to Your Zion once again. Take away, we pray, the itching for new doctrine, the long-ing for what is thought to be scientific and wise above what is written, and may Your church come to her moorings. May she cast anchor in the truth of God and there abide. If it is Your will, may we live to see brighter and better times.

If it might be so, we pray for our Lord to come very speedily to end these sluggish years, these long, delaying days. But if He does not come soon, put power into Your truth, and quicken Your church so that she may become energetic for the spread of Your Gospel, so that Your kingdom may come. First and above eve-rything, we seek the glory of God.

We ask for grace so that we may live with this end in view. May we lay our lives down for it. May this be our morning thought, and the thought that we have in our minds when we lie awake at night: What should I do, my Savior, to praise You? How can I make You illustrious and win another heart to Your throne?

Now bless us. Forgive our trespasses since we have sinned against You. Seal our pardon in our consciences, and make us feel that as we truly forgive those who trespass against us, so You have forgiven us all our iniquities. We pray that You do not lead us into temptation. Do not try us, Lord, or allow the Devil to try us. If we must be tried, then deliver us from evil, and especially from the evil one, so that he may get no dominion over us.

Oh, keep us, Lord. This life is so full of trials. Many are perplexed about temporary things. Do not let the enemy lead them to do or think anything amiss because of the difficulty of supply. Others are blessed with prosperity. Lord, do not let it be a curse to them. Let them know how to abound as well as to suffer loss (Philippians 4:12). In all things may they be instructed to glorify God, not only with all they are, but with all they have, and even with all they do not have. By a holy contentment, may they do without what it does not please You to bestow.

And then, Lord, give us day by day our daily bread. Provide for Your poor people. Do not let them think that the provision for them rests fully on themselves, but may they cry to You, for You have said of the person who lives righteously, *"Bread shall be given him; his waters shall be sure"* (Isaiah 33:16). If we follow You, if You lead us into a desert, You will scatter our path with manna. May Your people believe this, and let them have no care, but like the birds of the air, which neither sow nor gather into barns and yet are fed, so may Your people be (Matthew 6:26).

Above all, give us spiritual help. Give us wisdom, which is profitable to get. Give us the absence of all self-seeking and a complete yielding up of our desires to the will of God. Help us to be as Christ was, who was not His own, but gave Himself to His Father for our sins. Likewise, may we for His sake give ourselves up to do or suffer the will of our Father who is in heaven.

Remember Your people and their families, and convert their children. Give us help and strength. Spare precious lives that are in danger. Be gracious to any who are dying. May the life of God swallow up the death of the body. Prepare us all for Your glorious advent. Keep us waiting and watching, and do come quickly according to our hearts' desires, for we pray, *"Thy kingdom come. Thy will be done in earth, as it is in heaven....For thine is the kingdom, and the power, and the glory, for ever. Amen"* (Matthew 6:10, 13).

13

The Wings of Prayer

ur Father, Your children who know You delight themselves in Your presence. We are never happier than when we are near You. We have found a little heaven in prayer. It has eased our load to tell You of its weight. It has relieved our wound to tell You of its sting. It has restored our spirits to confess to You their wanderings. There is no place like the mercy seat for us.

We thank You, Lord, that not only have we found benefit in prayer, but we have been greatly enriched in the answers to it. You have opened Your hidden treasures to the voice of prayer. You have supplied our necessities as soon as we have cried unto You. Yes, we have found it true, *"Before they call, I will answer; and while they are yet speaking, I will hear"* (Isaiah 65:24).

We bless You, Lord, for instituting the blessed ordinance of prayer. What could we do without it? We take great shame to ourselves that we should use it so little. We pray that we may be people of prayer, taken up with it, that it may take us up and bear us up as on its wings toward heaven.

Now, hear the voice of our supplication. First, we ask at Your hands, great Father, complete forgiveness for all our trespasses and shortcomings. We hope we can say with truthfulness that from our hearts we forgive all those who have in any way trespassed against us. There does not lie in our hearts, we hope, any thought of enmity toward anyone. However we have been slandered or wronged, we want, with our innermost hearts, to forgive and forget all.

We come to You and pray that, for Jesus' sake, and through the virtue of the blood once *"shed for many for the remission of sins"* (Matthew 26:28), You would give us perfect pardon of every transgression. Blot out, Lord, all our sins like a cloud, and let them never be seen again. Grant us also the peace-speaking word of promise applied by the Holy Spirit, that *"being justified by faith, we have peace with God through our Lord Jesus Christ"* (Romans 5:1). Let us be forgiven and know it. May there remain no lingering question in our hearts about our reconciliation with God, but by a firm, full assurance based on faith in the finished work of Christ, may we stand as forgiven men and women against whom sin will never again be mentioned.

And then, Lord, we have another mercy to ask that is the burden of our prayer. It is that You would help us to live the lives that pardoned men should live. We have only a little time to remain here, for our lives are only a vapor; soon they vanish away. But we are most anxious that we may spend the time of our stay here in holy fear, that grace may be upon us from the beginning of our Christian lives even to the earthly close of them.

Lord, You know there are some who have not yet begun to live for You, and the prayer is now offered that they may today be born again. Others have lived in Your ways a long time and are not weary of them. We are sometimes surprised that You are not weary of us, but assuredly we delight ourselves in the ways of holiness more than we ever did. Oh, that our ways were directed to keep Your statutes without slip or flaw. We wish we were perfectly obedient in thought, word, and deed, entirely sanctified. We will never be satisfied until we wake up in Christ's likeness (Psalm 17:15), the likeness of perfection itself. Oh, work in us this same thing, we pray. May experience teach us more and more how to avoid occasions of sin. May we grow more watchful. May we have a greater supremacy over our own spirits. May we be able to control ourselves under all circumstances, and act in such a way that if the Master were to come at any moment, we would not be ashamed to give an account.

Lord, we are not what we want to be. This is our sorrow. Oh, that You would, by Your Spirit, help us in our walks of life to adorn the doctrine of God our Savior in all things. As businessmen, as working people, as parents, as children, as servants, as masters, whatever we may be, may we be such that Christ may look upon us with pleasure. May His joy be in us, for only then can our joy be full (John 15:11).

Dear Savior, we are Your disciples. You are teaching us the art of living, but we are very dull and very slow. Besides, there is such a bias in our corrupt nature, and there are such examples in the world, and the influence of an ungodly generation affects even those who know You. Oh, dear Savior, do not be impatient with us, but still school us at Your feet, until at last we will have learned some of the sublime lessons of self-sacrifice, meekness, humility, fervor, boldness, and love, which Your life is fit to teach us. O Lord, we implore You, mold us into Your own image. Let us live in You and live like You. Let us gaze upon Your glory until we are transformed by the sight and become Christlike among the sons of men.

Lord, hear the confessions of any who have backslidden, who are marring Your image rather than perfecting it. Hear the prayers of any who are conscious of great defects during the past. Give them peace of mind by pardon, but give them strength of mind also to keep clear of such mischief in the future. O Lord, we are sighing and crying more and more after You. The more we have of You, the more we want You. The more we grow like You, the more we perceive our defects, and the more we long for a higher standard, to reach even unto perfection itself.

Oh, help us! Spirit of the living God, continue to travail in us. Let the groanings that cannot be uttered continue to be within our spirits (Romans 8:26), for these are growing pains, and we will grow while we can sigh and cry, while we can confess and mourn. Yet this is not without a blessed hopefulness that He who *"hath begun a good work in* [us] *will perform it until the day of Jesus Christ"* (Philippians 1:6).

Bless, we pray, at this time, the entire church of God in every part of the earth. Prosper the work and service of Christian people, however they endeavor to spread the kingdom of Christ. Convert the heathen. Enlighten those who are in any form of error. Bring the entire church back to the original form of Christianity. Make her first pure, and then she will be united. Oh, Savior, let Your kingdom come. Oh, that You would reign and that Your will would *"be done in earth, as it is in heaven"* (Matthew 6:10)!

We ask You to use each and every one of us according to the ability we possess to be used. Take us, and let no talent lie dormant in the treasure-house, but may every pound of Yours be used in trading for You in the blessed market of soulwinning. Oh, give us success. Increase the gifts and graces of those who are saved. Bind us to one another in closer unity than ever. Let peace reign. Let holiness adorn us.

Hear us as we pray for all countries, and then for all sorts of people, from the sovereign on the throne to the peasant in the cottage. Let the blessing of heaven descend on men through Jesus Christ our Lord. Amen.

14

"Bless the Lord, O My Soul!"

Lord, we are longing to draw near to You. May Your Spirit draw us near. We come by the way of Christ our Mediator. We could not approach You, O God, if it were not for Him, but in Him we come boldly to the throne of heavenly grace (Hebrews 4:16). Nor can we come without thanksgiving— thanksgiving from the heart, such as the tongue can never express. You have chosen us from before the foundation of the world, and this wellspring of mercy sends forth streams of lovingkindness never ceasing. Because we were chosen, we have been redeemed with precious blood. Bless the Lord! We have been called by the Holy Spirit out of the world, and we have been led to obey that wondrous call that has quickened and renewed us, made us the people of God, and given us adoption into the divine family. Bless the Lord!

Our hearts want to pause as we remember the greatness of each one of Your favors, and we want to say, *"Bless the LORD, O my soul: and all that is within me, bless his holy name"* (Psalm 103:1). When we consider our utter unworthiness before conversion, and our great faultiness since, we cannot help but admire the riches of abounding grace that God has manifested to us unworthy ones. Bless the Lord!

When we think of all that You have promised to give, which our faith embraces as being really ours since the covenant makes it sure, we do not know how to proclaim abundantly enough the memory of Your grcat goodncss. We want to make our praises equal to our expectations, and our expectations equal to Your promises. We can never rise so high. We give to You, however, the praise of our entire being. Unto Jehovah, the God of Abraham, the God of Isaac, and the God of Jacob, the Creator of the world, the Redeemer of men, unto Jehovah be glory forever and ever, and let all His people praise Him. *"Let the redeemed of the LORD say so, whom he hath redeemed from the hand of the enemy"* (Psalm 107:2).

O Lord, Your works praise You, but Your saints bless You. This will be our heaven—our heaven of heavens eternally—to praise and magnify the great and ever blessed God. This day may many men and women break forth and say with the Virgin Mary, *"My soul doth magnify the Lord, and my spirit hath rejoiced in God my Saviour"* (Luke 1:46–47). This day may there go up sweet incense of praise laid privately by holy hands upon the altar of God. May the place be filled with the smoke of it, not perhaps to the consciousness of every one, but to the acceptance of God, who will smell a sweet savor of rest in Christ, and then in the praises of His people in Him.

But, Lord, when we praise You, we have to fold the wing. We have to cover the face and cover the feet and stand before You to worship in another fashion, for we confess that we are evil, evil in our nature. Though renewed by sovereign grace, Your people cannot speak of being clean, being rid of sin. There is sin that dwells in us that is our daily plague. O God, we humble ourselves before You. We ask that our faith may clearly perceive the blood of the atonement and the covering of the perfect righteousness of Christ. May we come afresh, depending alone on Jesus. "I the chief of sinners am, but Jesus died for me." May this be our one hope, that Jesus died and rose again, and that for His sake we are *"accepted in the beloved"* (Ephesians 1:6).

May every child of Yours have his conscience purged from dead works to serve the true and living God. May there be no cloud between us and our heavenly Father—not even a mist, not even the morning mist that is soon gone. May *"we walk in the light, as* [God] *is in the light"* (1 John 1:7). May our fellowship with the Father and with His Son, Jesus Christ, be unquestionable. May it be fuel. May it fill us with joy. May it be a most real fact this day. May we enjoy it to the full, knowing whom we have believed, knowing who is our Father, knowing who it is that dwells in us, even the Holy Spirit.

Take away from us everything that might hinder our delighting ourselves in God. May we come to God this day with supreme joy. May we speak of Him as "God, my exceeding joy, my own God is He." O God, give us a sense of belonging in You. May we come near to You, having no doubt and nothing whatsoever that would spoil the beautiful simplicity of a child-like faith that looks up into the great face of God and says, *"Our Father which art in heaven"* (Matthew 6:9).

There are those who have never repented of sin and have never believed in Christ, and consequently the wrath of God abides on them. They are living without God, living in darkness. O God, in Your great mercy, look upon them. They do not look at You, but may You look at them. May the sinner see his sin and mourn, see His Savior and accept Him, see himself saved, and go on his way rejoicing. Father, grant us this.

Once more we pray that You would bless Your church. Lord, quicken the spiritual lives of Your believers. You have given to Your church great activity, for which we thank You. May all of that outer activity and work be supported by a corresponding inner life. Do not let us get busy here and there with Martha, and forget to sit at Your feet with Mary (Luke 10:39–42).

Lord, restore to Your church the love of strong doctrine. May Your truth yet prevail. Purge out from among Your church those who would lead others away from the truth as it is in Jesus, and give back the old power and something more. Give us Pentecost—yes, many Pentecosts in one—and may we live to see Your church shine forth as clear as the sun, as fair as the moon, and as *"terrible as an army with banners"* (Song 6:4).

God, grant that we may live to see better days. But if perilous times should come in these last days, make us faithful. Raise up in England, raise up in Scotland, men who will hold the truth firmly as their fathers did. In every country where there has been a faithful church, raise up men who will not let the ship drift upon the rocks. O God of the judges, You who did raise up first one and then another when the people went astray from God, raise up for us still (for our Joshuas are dead) Deborahs, Baraks, Gideons, Jephthahs, and Samuels, who will maintain for God His truth and defeat the enemies of Israel. Lord, look upon Your church in these days. Lord, revive us. Lord, restore us. Lord, give power to Your

Word again so that Your name may be glorified in all the earth.

Remember the church of God in this land in all its various phases and portions, and pour out Your Spirit upon it. Remember the multitude of Your people across the sea in America; prosper them and bless them with Your increase. Wherever You have a people, may Jesus dwell with them and reveal Himself to His own for Christ's sake, to whom be glory with the Father and with the Holy Spirit, forever and ever. Amen.

15

"He Ever Liveth"

Our God, we come to You by Jesus Christ, who has gone within the veil on our behalf and *ever liveth to make intercession for* [us]" (Hebrews 7:25). Our poor prayers could never reach You if it were not for Him, but His hands are full of sweet perfume, which makes our pleading sweet to You. His blood is sprinkled on the mercy seat, and now we know that You always hear those who approach You through that ever blessed name.

We have deeply felt our entire unworthiness even to lift up our eyes to the place where Your honor dwells. You have made us die to our self-righteousness. We pray now because we have been quickened. We have received a new life, and the breath of that life is prayer. We have risen from the dead, and we make intercession through the life that Christ has given us. We plead with the living God with living hearts because He has made us alive.

Our first prayer is for those who do not pray. There is an ancient promise of Yours that says, *"I am found of them that sought me not: I said, Behold me, behold me, unto a nation that was not called by my name"* (Isaiah 65:1). Prove the sovereignty of Your grace, the priority of Your power, which runs before the will of man, by making many willing in this, the day of Your power. Call *"those things which be not as though they were"* (Romans 4:17). May the day come soon in which they who are in their graves will hear the voice of God, and those who hear will live.

How often You show Your mighty power. O Lord, we bless You that the voice of God has called many to Christ. Those who are hardened have felt a softness stealing over their spirits. Those who were careless have been compelled to sit down and think. Those that were wrapped up in earthly things have been compelled to think of eternal things. Thinking, they have been disturbed and driven to despair, but afterward led to You, even to You, dear Savior, who was lifted high upon the cross so that by Your death sinners might live.

But, Lord, we next pray that Your own people would know the quickening of the Spirit of God. Lord, we thank You for the very least life in God, for the feeblest ray of faith and glimmering of hope. We are glad to see anything of Christ in any man, but You have come, O Savior, not only that we might have life, but that we might have it more abundantly (John 10:10), so our prayer is that there may be abundance of life.

Make Your people *"strong in the Lord, and in the power of his might"* (Ephesians 6:10). Lord, we find when we walk close to You that we have no desire for the world. When we get away altogether from the things that are seen and temporal, and live upon the invisible and eternal (2 Corinthians 4:18), then we have angels' food—better than that, the food of Christ Himself, for his flesh is meat indeed, and His blood is drink indeed (John 6:55). Then we have meat to eat that the world does not know about. We ask You to raise all our brothers and sisters in Christ into the high and heavenly frame of mind in which they will be *in* the world and not be *of* it. Whether they have little or much of temporal things, may they be rich in You and full of joy in the Holy Spirit, and so be blessed men and women.

We pray for some of Your own people who seem to be doing very little for You. Lord, have mercy on those whose strength runs toward the world, and who give but little of their strength to the spreading of the Gospel and the winning of souls. Oh, let none of us fritter away our existence. May we begin to live since Christ has died. May we reckon that because He died, we died to all the world, and because He lives, we live in newness of life. Lord, we thank You for that newness of life.

We praise Your name for a new heaven and a new earth. We bless You that we now see what we never saw before and hear what we never heard before. Oh, may we enter into the very secret place of this inner life. May we have as much grace as can be obtained. May we become perfect after the manner of Your servant Paul, but still press forward, still seeking to be more and more conformed to the image of Christ.

Lord, make us useful. Oh, let no believer live for himself. May we be trying to bring others to Christ. May our fellow workers and neighbors all know how we live. If they do not understand the secret of that life, may they still see the fruit of that life and ask, "What is this?" May they inquire their way to Christ, and may they be sanctified, too.

O Lord, we ask You to visit Your church. May none of us imagine that we are living uprightly unless we are bringing others to the Cross. Oh, keep us from worldliness. Keep us much in prayer. Keep us with the light of God shining down upon us. May we be a happy people, not because we are screened from affliction, but because we are walking in the light of God.

Again, we offer prayer for the many efforts that are scattered abroad today. May they do good wherever they are. We pray for all churches. Lord, revive them all. Wherever Christ is preached, may it be proved that He draws all men unto Himself. May the preaching of Christ today be especially effective. Oh, that You would raise up many who would preach Christ, simply, boldly, and with the Holy Spirit sent down from heaven. Send us better days. Send us days of refreshing, straight from Your presence.

Lord, shake the earth with Your power. Oh, that the heathen lands may hear the Word of God and live! But first convert the church, and then You will convert the world. Oh, deal with those who depart from the faith and grieve Your Holy Spirit. Bring them back again to their first love. May Christ be fully and faithfully preached everywhere to the glory of His name. Now forgive us every iniquity, and lift us beyond the power of every sin. Lift us into heavenly places to pray and praise You. Make our homes full of sacred power.

Last of all, come, Lord Jesus. This is the great cry of our souls. Even so, come quickly, come quickly, Lord Jesus. Amen (Revelation 22:20).

16

The Great Sacrifice

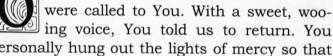Father God, we well remember when we were called to You. With a sweet, wooing voice, You told us to return. You personally hung out the lights of mercy so that we might know the way home. Your dear Son Himself came down to seek us. But we wandered still. It brings tears to our eyes to think that we were so foolish and wicked, for we often extinguished the light within. Conscience we tried to harden. We sinned against light and knowledge with a high hand against our God.

You often brought us very low, even to our knees. We cried for mercy, but we rose to sin again. Blessed was that day when You struck the blow of grace—that effective blow. Then You withered up our splendor, and all our perfection was rolled in the dust. We saw ourselves slain by the law, lost, ruined, and undone. Then we rolled to and fro in the tempests of our thoughts, staggering like drunken men at our wits' end. Then we cried unto You in our trouble. Blessed be Your name forever, for You delivered us.

Oh, what a happy day that sealed our pardon with the precious blood of Jesus accepted by faith! We recall the memory of that blessed season by repeating it. We come again to the cross whereon the Savior bled. We give another look of faith to Him. We trust we never take our eyes off Him, but if we have done so, we want to look anew. We want to gaze upon the body of the Son of God, pierced with nails, parched with thirst, bleeding, dying, because *"it pleased the LORD to bruise him; he hath put him to grief"* (Isaiah 53:10).

Lord God, we see in Your crucified Son a sacrifice for sin. We see how You have *"made him to be sin for us...that we might be made the righteousness of God in him"* (2 Corinthians 5:21). We again accept Him to be everything to us. This is the victim by whose blood the covenant is made through faith. This is the Passover Lamb by the sprinkling of whose blood all Israel is secured. You have said, *"When I see the blood, I will pass over you"* (Exodus 12:13). This is the blood that gives us access into what is within the veil. This is the blood that is now drink indeed to our souls. We rejoice in the joy that this new wine of the covenant has given to our spirits.

We want to take afresh the cup of salvation and call upon the name of the Lord. We want to pay our vows now in the midst of all the Lord's people and in the courts of His house. This is a part of the payment of our vows—that we bless the Lord Jesus, who has put away our sin. We bless Him that He has redeemed us unto Himself, not with corruptible things such as silver and gold, but with His own precious blood (1 Peter 1:18–19).

We again declare ourselves today to be the Lord's. We are not our own; we are bought with a price (1 Corinthians 6:19–20). Lord Jesus, renew Your grasp of us; take us over again. With even greater speed than ever before, we surrender ourselves to You, and so *"bind the sacrifice with cords, even unto the horns of the altar"* (Psalm 118:27). Lord, I am Your servant, and the son of Your handmaid. You have loosed my bonds. The Lord lives! Blessed be my Rock. From now on I hide myself within that Rock. For Him I live.

May the Lord enable all His people to give themselves up to Jesus again with sincere and undivided hearts. Lord, place in us anew the marks and tokens of Your possession, until every one of us who can will say, *"From henceforth let no man trouble me: for I bear in my body the marks of the Lord Jesus"* (Galatians 6:17).

We bless You, Lord, for that mark to which some of us can look back with much joy. It is not on our hands alone, nor on our foreheads alone, nor on our feet alone, nor on our hearts alone. Our whole bodies have been buried with Christ in baptism unto death (Romans 6:4). By our willing consecration, our whole bodies, souls, and spirits belong to Christ from now on and forever.

Our Father, there is one prayer that has kept rising to my lips even while I have been talking with You. It comes from my very heart. It is that You would bring others to Yourself. O God of Jacob, have You not said, *"Yet will I gather others to him, beside those that are gathered unto him"* (Isaiah 56:8)? Have You not given to Your Son the heathen for His inheritance, and the uttermost parts of the earth for His possession (Psalm 2:8)? Lord, give Your Son the reward of His travail. Give Him a part of that reward this day wherever He is preached. Oh, that some might be moved with the love of Christ.

Lord, some do not know who You are. Convince them of Your deity and Your power to save. Lord, many of them do not think. They live as if there will be an end to them when they die. O divine Spirit, convince them of judgment to come. Set before each careless eye that day of terrible splendor when all people must give an account for every idle word that they have spoken (Matthew 12:36). O divine Spirit, teach unreasonable men true reason. Teach the callous sensitivity. Look upon them, Jesus, just as You did on those of the synagogue, not with anger, but with grief because of the hardness of their hearts. Cry again, *"Father, forgive them; for they know not what they do"* (Luke 23:34). Bring many, many this very day to Your dear feet that were nailed to the cross. How we long for this. Deny us what You will, only bring sinners to Yourself.

Lord Jesus, You are gone from us. We rejoice that this is the fact, for You have taught us that it was to our advantage that You went, and that the Comforter would be with us. But, Lord, let us not miss that promised presence of the Comforter. May He be here to help us in all works of faith and labors of love, and may we feel that He has come among us and is dwelling with us because He is convincing the world of sin, of righteousness, and of judgment to come (John 16:7–8).

O Spirit of God, bring men to accept the great propitiation, to see their sin washed away in the crimson flood whose fount was opened when the heart of Christ was pierced. May blood-washed sinners begin to sing on earth that everlasting anthem that will be sung by all the redeemed in heaven.

We implore You now, Lord, to look upon all Your people, and grant every one a blessing. Some are in great trouble. Deliver them, we pray. Others may be in great peril, though they have no trouble. May the Lord save His people from the evils of prosperity. It may be that some of Your own people find it hard to worship because of cares. May they be able, like

Abraham, when the birds came down upon the sacrifice, to drive them away.

O Spirit of God, make us all more holy. Work in us more completely the image of Christ. We long to be like the Lord Jesus Christ in spirit and character and in unselfishness of life. Give us the character of Christ, we pray. Redemption from the power of sin is purchased with His blood, and we crave for it. We pray that we may daily receive it. Let the whole militant church of Christ be blessed.

Put power into all faithful ministries. Convert this country; save it from abounding sin. Let all the nations of the earth know the Lord, but especially bless those nations where our Lord Jesus is worshiped this day in the same fashion.

May the Lord bless His people. Bring the church to break down all bonds of nationality, all limits of sects, and may we feel the blessed unity that is the very glory of the church of Christ. Let the whole earth be filled with His glory. Our prayer can never cease until we reach this point: *Thy kingdom come. Thy will be done in earth, as it is in heaven"* (Matthew 6:10). Nothing less than this can we ask for.

Now hear us as we pray for those in government and all in authority, and ask Your blessing to rest upon this land. Let Your blessing extend over all the family of man. We ask it for Christ's sake. Amen.

17

Oh, for More Grace!

ur Father, You do hear us when we pray. You have provided an Advocate and Intercessor in heaven now. We cannot come to You unless Your Holy Spirit gives us the desire and helps us while we plead. May we know Christ and have Him to be our all in all. He is everything to us. More than all we find in Him. We do accept You, Lord Jesus, to be *"made unto us wisdom, and righteousness, and sanctification, and redemption"* (1 Corinthians 1:30). We will not look outside of You for anything, for everything is in You. Our sin is pardoned. Our sinful nature is subdued. We have a perfect righteousness. We have an immortal life. We have a sure hope. We have an immovable foundation. Why should we look beyond You? Why should we look within to ourselves, knowing that You are the only well from which we will draw living water, the only foundation upon which we will be built? We want to thrust out new roots this day, and take a fresh hold on the blessed soil in which grace has planted us.

O Savior, reveal Yourself anew; teach us a little more; help us to go a little deeper into the divine mysteries. May we grip You and grasp You. May we draw from You the nourishment for our spirits. May we be in You as a branch is in the tree, and may we bear fruit from You. Without You, we can do nothing.

Forgive Your servants, we pray, for any wanderings during the past. If we have forgotten You, do not forget us. If we have acted apart from You, forgive the act. Blot out the sin. Help us in the future to live only in You, to speak, and even to think, only in union with our living Head. Take away from us all life that is contrary to the life of Christ. Bring us into complete subjection in Him, until for us to live is Christ in every single act of life. May we walk humbly with God in joyful faith in the finished work of Christ.

Savior, look on Your beloved ones, and give blessings according to our necessities. We cannot pray a prayer that would comprise all, but You, our Great Intercessor, can plead for each one and get for each one of us the blessing wanted. Are we depressed? Give us stronger faith. Have we become worldly? Pardon this great offense, and lead us back into spiritual things. Have we become joyous but have forgotten the Source of joy? Lord, sweeten and savor that joy with the sweet perfume of Your own presence. Are we to preach but feel weak? Oh, be our strength. Are we involved in the Sunday school program and have seen little success? Lord, teach us how to teach. Give us our boys and girls as our spiritual reward. Are we sick? Do we have those who vex us because they are unholy and ungodly? This, indeed, is a terrible trial to many. Lord, help them, both in their personal sickness and in this great spiritual trouble. Do we have dear ones whom we love with all our hearts who languish before our eyes? Lord, have pity on them; restore them, and give them patience to bear pain. Give us resignation to Your will in this matter. Whatever the trial of Your servants, make a way of escape that we may be able to bear it (1 Corinthians 10:13).

Our great concern, however, is to grow in grace and to become like our Master. We struggle and struggle, but how small is our progress! Lord, help us in any matter in which we have felt defeated. If we have been betrayed through lack of watchfulness, Lord, forgive and help another time. If any of Your servants have lost the brightness of their evidence, lead them to come to Christ as sinners if they cannot come as saints. And if, through Satan's temptation, any are sorely pressed even to keep standing, hold them up. If any have fallen, help them to say, *"Rejoice not against me, O mine enemy: when I fall, I shall arise"* (Micah 7:8).

Now, look in great mercy on those who are unconverted. Lord, save them. Some are quite careless. Lord, they are dead. Come and quicken them. We cannot see, but You can. Oh, that some of the most callous and hardened might be softened by the touch of Your Spirit this very day. Others who are not careless, who are seeking eternal life, but who are going the wrong way, the way of works, may they be shown their error; may they be led in the way by You; may they look, and, looking, live. We know how many of them are wanting to be this and that before they take Christ to be all in all. May they cease their seeking by finding everything in Christ. Since You are a prayer-hearing God, and a God of pardon, issue many a pardon from Your heavenly court today, sealed with the Redeemer's blood, signed with the Father's name. Oh, today, Lord, before men grow old in sin, before they die in their sins, save them with an everlasting salvation.

God, bless our country and our sovereign. God, bless this city. May there be no disquiet between the different orders of men—the employer and the employed—but may there be a general spirit of goodwill given to the people of this city, and may You prosper us.

Remember all people, especially the poor, the widows, and the fatherless, and any who are depressed in spirit, whose depression tends toward the failure of reason. Lord, restore them, and those who are dying. O Lord, do not let them die without hope. May Your believing people learn to pass away without even tasting the bitterness of death. May they enter into rest, each one walking in his own uprightness (Isaiah 57:2).

Save this age from its own intellectual pride. Give back the spirit of simple faith in Christ, for we desire His glory. *"For thine is the kingdom, and the power, and the glory, for ever. Amen"* (Matthew 6:13).

18

The Peace of God

ur God, we do not stand far away as Israel did in Sinai, nor does a dark veil hang between Your face and ours, but the veil has been torn by the death of our divine Lord and Mediator, Jesus Christ. In His name, we come to the mercy seat all sprinkled with blood. Here we present our prayers and our praises, accepted in Him.

We confess that we are guilty. We bow our heads and confess that we have broken Your law and the covenant of which it is a part. If You were to deal with us under the covenant of works, none of us could stand. We must confess that we deserve Your wrath and to be banished forever from Your presence. But You have made a new covenant, and we come under its divine shadow. We come in the name of Jesus. He is our High Priest. He is our righteousness. He is the Well Beloved in whom You, O Lord, are well pleased.

Holy Spirit, teach us how to pray. Let us know how to pray as we should. Our first prayer is, "May You be adored and reign over the whole earth. Blessed be Your name." We desire to see all men submit themselves to Your gracious government. We desire especially that there may be an intense love for You and a perfect obedience to You in the hearts of Your own. Grant this to each of us. May each one of us pray, "Lord, sanctify me. Make me obedient. Write Your law upon my heart and upon my mind." Make our natures so pure that temptation cannot defile us.

"Lead us not into temptation, but deliver us from evil" (Matthew 6:13). May our courses be very clean; may our paths be very straight. May we keep our garments unspotted from the world. In thought, desire, and imagination, in will and in purpose, may we be holy, for God is holy (Leviticus 11:44).

O God, we pray again, fulfill that covenant promise, *"I will take away the stony heart out of your flesh, and I will give you an heart of flesh"* (Ezekiel 36:26). May we be very tender toward You. May we feel Your faintest admonition. May even the gentlest breath of Your Spirit suffice to move us. May we not be *"as the horse, or as the mule, which have no understanding: whose mouth must be held in with bit and bridle, lest they come near unto thee"* (Psalm 32:9), but may we be like children who are obedient to their father. May we cheerfully yield our members to be *"instruments of right-eousness"* (Romans 6:13). May we have natural desires worked in our new nature for all that is pure and honest, unselfish and Christlike.

Oh, Spirit of God, dwell in us. Is this not also a covenant promise: *"I will put my spirit within you, and cause you to walk in my stat-utes"* (Ezekiel 36:27)? Dwell within us, Holy Spirit. Govern over us, Holy Spirit. Transform us into Your own likeness, O Holy Spirit! Then we will be clean; then we will keep the law. We want to offer a prayer to You for those who are quite foreign to the work of the Spirit of God, who have never owned their God, who have lived as if there were no God. Open their eyes so that they may see God, even though that sight should make them tremble and wish to die. Oh, let none of us live without our God and Father. Take away our hearts of stone; take away the frivolities, the foolishness, the giddiness of our youth, and give us the ability to earnestly seek true joy where it can alone be found—in reconciliation to God and conformity to His will.

O Lord God, save the careless; save the sinful. Take away the drunkard from his drink. Deliver the unholy and unjust men from their filthiness. Renew the lives of the dishonest and false. O Spirit of God, renew any who are lov-ers of pleasure, who are dead while they live, and any who are lovers of self, whose lives are bound by the narrowness of their own being.

Lord God, regenerate them; make them new creatures in Christ.

God the Holy Spirit, may faith grow in men. May they believe in Christ unto the saving of their souls. May their little faith brighten into strong faith, and may their strong faith ripen into the full assurance of faith. May we all have this last blessing. May we believe God fully, and may we never waver. Resting in the Great Surety and High Priest of the New Covenant, may we feel *"the peace of God, which passeth all understanding"* (Philippians 4:7), and may we enter into Your rest.

Bless Your people who are at rest, and deepen that rest. May the rest that You give be further enhanced by the rest that they find when they take Your yoke upon them and learn from You (Matthew 11:29). May Your Word be very sweet to them. May there come over our spirits a deep calm, as when Christ hushed both winds and waves. May we feel not only resignation to Your will, but delight in it, and pleasure in all the Lord provides. May we rest in our God and be quite happy in the thought that You remember our sins and our iniquities no more. You have brought us into covenant with Yourself by a covenant that can never fail. Therefore, like David, may we say, *"Although my house be not so with God; yet he hath made with me an everlasting covenant, ordered in all things, and sure"* (2 Samuel 23:5).

Lord, bless Your Word throughout the world. Prosper all missionary efforts among the heathen, all work among the Islamic nations. And send Your grace to the churches at home. Turn the current of thought that is set so strongly in the wrong direction, and bring men to love the simplicities of the Gospel. Remember our country in great mercy, and may You give the blessing to all ranks and conditions of men. May multitudes come to Christ from among the poorest of the poor. Let the wealthy be led away from their sin and brought to Jesus' feet. Be gracious to the sovereign and royal family and to all who are in authority over us. May peace and order be maintained, and do not let the peace of the world be broken.

But what of all this? Our hearts go far beyond all this: *"Thy will be done in earth, as it is in heaven....For thine is the kingdom, and the power, and the glory, for ever"* (Matthew 6:10, 13). Come, Lord Jesus; come quickly (Revelation 22:20). All things are in Your hand. Come quickly. The cries of Your people persuade You; *"the Spirit and the bride say, Come"* (Revelation 22:17). O our Redeemer, do not delay. To the Father, to the Son, and to the Holy Spirit, the God of Abraham, and the God of our Lord Jesus Christ, be glory forever and ever. Amen.

19

To Be like Christ

lessed are You, O God. Teach us Your statutes! Because You are the infinitely blessed One, You can impart blessing, and You are infinitely willing to do so. Therefore, we approach You with great confidence through Jesus Christ Your Son, whom You have made blessed forevermore.

O Lord, hear the voice of Your servants this day. According to Your infinite love and wisdom, *"according to* [Your] *riches in glory by Christ Jesus"* (Philippians 4:19), answer us.

First, we want to confess before You, O God, the sin we have committed, mourning over it. Touch each one now with such tenderness of heart that every one of us may lament that You should have even a few things against us, if they are only a few. In the great love of our blessed Master, He said to His churches, *"Notwithstanding I have a few things against thee"* (Revelation 2:20). O Lord, if You have so kept us by Your grace that there have been only a few things against us, still help us to mourn much over them. Oh, Infinite Love, can we sin against You at all? How debased is our nature then! Forgive, sweet Savior; forgive sins against Your love and blood, against Your wounds and death. Give us Your Spirit, O Savior, more fully, so that we may live Your life while we are here among the sons of men. As You are, even so also are we in this world, and we want the parallel to become more close and perfect every day!

Forgive those who have never felt the guilt of sin, who live in it, who are carnally minded, who are therefore dead. Quicken them by Your divine Spirit. Take away the pleasure that they feel in sin. Deliver them from being the bond slaves of it. Alas, we know the sorrow of some-times being captured by it, but still we are not yet slaves. The Spirit, the life of God in Jesus Christ, has made us *"free from the law of sin and death"* (Romans 8:2). Deliver sinners, Lord. Bring them up out of the horrible pit. Deliver them from the death of their nature, and save them by the Spirit of the living God. Apply the precious blood of Jesus to their hearts and minds.

Lord, hear us who are Your children, in whom *"the Spirit itself beareth witness with our spirit, that we are the children of God"* (Romans 8:16). Hear us while we bring before You our daily struggles. Blessed be Your name! There are some sins that You have helped us overcome, and now they are trodden beneath our feet with many a tear that we ever should have been in bondage to them. But there are rebellions within our nature still. We think that we are becoming holy, and behold, we discover that we are under the power of pride, that we are self-conceited. Lord, help us to master pride.

When we try to be humble before You, we find ourselves falling into idleness and inactivity. Lord, slay sloth within us, and never let us find a pillow of ease in the doctrines of grace while a single sin still remains. Besides, great God, the raging lusts of the flesh sometimes pounce on us like wild beasts. Help us to be watchful so that we are not torn and wounded by them. Keep us, Lord, for without Your keeping, we cannot keep ourselves.

Alas, we are even sometimes subject to unbelief. If trials come that we do not expect or if our bodies grow faint, how liable we are to begin to doubt the faithful promise and thereby grieve the Holy Spirit. Lord, we cannot bear this. It is not enough for us that our garments are clean and that we walk uprightly before men. We long to walk before You in such a way that nothing would grieve Your Spirit, nothing would vex the tender love of our Beloved. Come, divine Spirit, and exercise Your cleansing power upon us according to Your promise, *"I will cleanse their blood that I have not cleansed: for the* LORD *dwelleth in Zion"* (Joel 3:21).

Oh, that everything might help us toward purity, for we crave it. We attend the things of the Spirit, and there is groaning within us to be utterly delivered from the things of the flesh, so that we may be a cleansed temple in spirit, soul, and body, fit for the indwelling of the Holy One of Israel. Lord, help us, we pray, in our daily lives, to be as Christ was. If we are men of sorrows, may there be the same luster to our sorrow that there was to His, in patience and holy submission to divine law. If we are men of activity, may our work be like His, for He *"went about doing good"* (Acts 10:38). In all ways, may we seek the good of our fellowmen and the glory of our God.

We wish that the zeal for Your house would consume us. We pray that we would be full of sacred warmth. We desire that our lips would be touched with a live coal so that a fire would be perpetually flaming and burning in us. We want to be living sacrifices unto God.

Bless us, we pray, in the areas of our example and influence. May we always have a beneficial effect on others. May there be a sweetness and a light about us that all must be obliged to perceive. We do not crave this for our own honor, but so that our light may *"so shine before men, that they may see* [our] *good works, and glorify* [our] *Father which is in heaven"* (Matthew 5:16). Lord, grant us this!

Bless the unconverted among us. Bring them in, dear Savior; bring them in. Help the saved among us to *"compel them to come in, that* [Your] *house may be filled"* (Luke 14:23). May a sacred compulsion be used so that they may not be left outside to starve in the highways and hedges, but be brought in to the gospel feast.

Lord, bless our country at this time. May You be gracious to those who have the helm of affairs so that in the midst of great difficulty they may be wisely and graciously directed. God, bless those in government with every mercy, and let all who are in authority share the divine favor. Bless other countries, too, for whom we most earnestly pray, especially for our family in Christ across the Atlantic. We bless and praise You that we have so many there who are not only of our own kin by nationality, but also kin in Christ. God bless them, as well as those in the South Seas. Lord, bless the church of Christ there. Remember the struggling ones on the continent of Europe, and all the missionaries who are laboring in foreign fields.

Oh, Savior, let Your kingdom come. When will this earth be delivered from superstition and unbelief? May You hear creation's groans and come quickly. O great Deliverer, You are the joy of the earth. You are still the expected of the tribes of Israel. Come, we pray, absent love, dear unknown, fairest of ten thousand, come a second time to earth to the sons of men, and especially to Your bride, the church. Even so, come quickly, Lord Jesus. Amen (Revelation 22:20).

20

The Look of Faith

ur Father, we have listened to Your gracious words. Truly Your paths overflow with abundance. Wherever You are, mercy abounds. Before Your feet, rivers of grace spring up. When You come to man, it is with the fullness of pardoning love. You bid us to come and seek You while You may be found (Isaiah 55:6). We come now. May Your Holy Spirit help us. May Jesus lead the way and be our Mediator now!

Blessed be Your name! There are many who sought Your face years ago. Since then, we have tasted that You are gracious, and we know by delightful experience that You do indeed give milk and honey to those who trust You. Oh, we wish we had known You earlier.

Lord, You have been full of truth and faithfulness to us throughout every step of our journey, and though You have not withheld the rod of the covenant from us, we are as grateful for that now as for the kisses of Your lips. You have dealt well with Your servants according to Your Word (Psalm 119:65). Blessed be Your name forever and ever.

But there are some who have never come to You. They are hearers, but hearers only. They have listened to gracious invitations thousands of times, but they have never accepted them. Say to them, "You have gone this far, but you will proceed no further in your carelessness and trifling. Here you will stay and turn to your God." O Savior, You have all power in heaven and earth; therefore, You can, through the preaching of Your Word, influence the hearts of men. Turn them, and they will be turned. Oh, do it this day, Lord.

We want to come to You now in our prayers. As we came at first, we want to come again. We want to renew our vows, we want to repeat our repentance and our faith, and then look at the bronze serpent and touch the hem of Your garment. We want to begin again. O Lord, help us to do it in sincerity and truth. First, we confess that we are by nature lost and by practice ruined. *"We are all as an unclean thing, and all our righteousnesses are as filthy rags"* (Isaiah 64:6). We want to lie at those dear pierced feet, bleeding at heart because of sin, wounded, mangled, crushed by the Fall and by our transgression. We confess that if You were to number our sins against us and deal with us accordingly, we would be sent to the lowest hell.

We have no merit, no claim, no righteousness of our own. Now, dear Savior, we look to You. Oh, that some might look for the first time. Oh, that those of us who have long looked would fix our happy gaze again upon that blessed substitutionary sacrifice in whom is all our hope. Dear Savior, we do take You to be everything to us, our Sin-Bearer and our Sin-Destroyer. We do not have a shadow of a hope anywhere but in You—Your life, Your death, Your resurrection, Your ascension, Your glory, Your reign, Your second advent. These are the only stars in our sky.

We look up to You and are filled with light. But, oh, dear, dear Savior, we dare not turn to ordinances. We dare not turn to our own prayers and tears and almsgiving. We dare not look to our own works. We only look to You. Your wounds, Emmanuel, bleed the balm that heals our wounds. Your head once crowned with thorns, Your body once laid in the silent tomb, Your Godhead once covered and concealed from man but now resplendent amid triumphant hosts—these we gaze upon.

If we must perish trusting in You, we must perish. But we know we cannot, for You have bound up our salvation with Your glory, and because You are a glorious Savior forever, none who trust in You will ever be ashamed (Psalm 34:22).

We do trust You now. If all our past experience has been a mistake, we will begin at the Cross today. If we have never had any experience of You before, we would begin today. Oh, hear, Lord, hear our prayer:

> Dear Savior, draw reluctant hearts;
> To You let sinners fly.

By Christ's agony and bloody sweat, by His cross and passion, by His precious death and burial, we implore You, hear us now! We plead with You for some who are not pleading for themselves. O Spirit of God, do not let it be so any longer. Sweetly use Your key to open the locked door and come into men's hearts and dwell there so that they may live.

We have a thousand things to ask. We would like to plead for our country and for all countries. We would like to plead with You for the sick and for the dying, for the poor and for the fatherless. We have innumerable blessings to ask, but somehow they all fade away from our prayer just now, and this is our one cry: "Save, Lord, we pray. Even now send salvation! Come, Holy Spirit, to open blind eyes and unstop deaf ears and quicken dead hearts."

Father, glorify Your Son so that Your Son may glorify You. Holy Spirit, take of these things of Christ and reveal them unto us. We gather all our prayers in that salvation through the blood of the Lamb. Amen.

21

Boldness at the Throne of Grace

God! We do not want to speak to You as from a distance, or stand like trembling Israel under the law at a distance from the burning mount. We have not come to Mount Sinai, but to Mount Zion, and that is a place for holy joy and thankfulness, not for terror and bondage. Blessed be Your name, O Lord! We have learned to call You *"our Father which art in heaven"* (Matthew 6:9). There is reverence, for You are in heaven. But there is sweet familiarity, for You are our Father.

We want to draw very near to You now through Jesus Christ the Mediator, and we want to be bold to speak to You as a man speaks with his friend. Have You not said by Your Spirit, *"Let us therefore come boldly unto the throne of grace"* (Hebrews 4:16)? We might well flee from Your face if we only remembered our sinfulness. Lord, we do remember it with

125

shame and sorrow. We are grieved to think we have offended You and have neglected Your sweet love and tender mercy so long. But we have *"now returned unto the Shepherd and Bishop of* [our] *souls"* (1 Peter 2:25). Led by such grace, we look to Him whom we crucified. We have mourned for Him and then have mourned for our sin.

Now, Lord, we confess our guilt before You with tenderness of heart. We pray that You would seal home to every believer that full and free, that perfect and irreversible charter of forgiveness that You gave to all who put their trust in Jesus Christ. Lord, You have said, *"If we confess our sins,* [You are] *faithful and just to forgive us our sins, and to cleanse us from all unrighteousness"* (1 John 1:9). There is the sin confessed. There is the ransom accepted. Therefore, we know we have peace with God, and we bless that glorious One who has come *"to finish the transgression, and to make an end of sins, and...to bring in everlasting righteousness"* (Dan. 9:24), which by faith we take unto ourselves and You impute unto us.

Now, Lord, will You be pleased to cause all Your children's hearts to dance within them for joy? Oh, help Your people to come to Jesus again today. May we be looking unto Him now as we did at first. May we never take our eyes away from His divine person, from His infinite merit, from His finished work, from His living power, or from the expectancy of His speedy coming to *"judge the world with righteousness, and the people with his truth"* (Psalm 96:13).

Bless all Your people with some special gift. If we might make a choice of one, it would be this: *"Quicken* [us] *according to thy word"* (Psalm 119:25). We have life. Give it to us more abundantly. Oh, that we might have so much life that out of the midst of us there might *"flow rivers of living water"* (John 7:38). Lord, make us useful. Dear Savior, use the very least among us. Take the one talent and let it be invested for interest for the great Father. May it please You to show each one of us what You would have us to do. In our families, in our businesses, in the walks of ordinary life, may we be serving the Lord. May we often speak a word for His name and help in some way to scatter the light among the ever growing darkness. Before we go to be with You, may we have sown some seed that we will bring with us on our shoulders in the form of sheaves of blessing.

Lord God, bless our Sunday schools, and give a greater interest in such work, so that there may be no lack of men and women who are glad and happy in teaching the young. Impress this, we pray, upon Your people just now. Move men who have gifts and ability to preach the Gospel. There are many who live in villages, and there is no preaching of the Gospel near them. Lord, set them to preaching themselves. May You move some hearts so powerfully that their tongues cannot be quiet any longer, and may they attempt in some way, either personally or by supporting someone, to bring the Gospel into dark, benighted hamlets so that the people may know the truth.

O Lord, stir up the dwellers in this great, great city. Arouse us to the spiritual destitution of the masses. O God, help us all by some means, by any means, by every means, to get at the ears of men for Christ's sake so that we may reach their hearts. We send up an exceedingly great and sorrowful cry to You on behalf of the millions who enter no place of worship, but rather violate its sanctity and despise its blessed message. Lord, wake up London, we implore You. Send us another Jonah. Send us another John the Baptist. Oh, that Christ Himself would send forth multitudes of laborers among this thick-standing corn, for *"the harvest truly is plenteous, but the labourers are few"* (Matthew 9:37). O God! Save this city; save this country; save all countries, and let Your kingdom come. May every knee bow, and may all confess that Jesus Christ is Lord (Philippians 2:10–11).

Our most earnest prayers go up to heaven to You now for great sinners, for men and women who are polluted and depraved by the filthiest of sins. With sovereign mercy make a raid among them. Come and capture some of these so that they may become great lovers of

Him who forgives them, and may they become great champions for the Cross.

Lord, look upon the multitudes of rich people in this city who know nothing about the Gospel and do not wish to know. Oh, that somehow the spiritually poor might be rich with the Gospel of Jesus Christ. And then, Lord, look upon the multitude of the poor and the working classes who think religion is a perfectly unnecessary thing for them. By some means, we pray, get them to think and bring them to listen, for *"faith cometh by hearing, and hearing by the word of God"* (Romans 10:17).

Above all, O Holy Spirit, descend more mightily. O God, flood the land until there are streams of righteousness. Is there not a promise that says, *"I will pour water upon him that is thirsty, and floods upon the dry ground"* (Isaiah 44:3)? Lord, set Your people praying. Stir up the church to greater prayerfulness.

Now, as You have told us to do, we pray for the people among whom we dwell. We pray for those in authority in the land, asking every blessing for those in government; Your guidance and direction for the Parliament; and Your blessing to all judges and rulers and also upon the poorest of the poor and the lowest of the low. Lord, bless the people. *"Let the people praise thee, O God; let all the people praise thee"* (Psalm 67:3), for Jesus Christ's sake. Amen.

22

The Presence of the Word

ur Father in heaven, our hearts are full of gratitude to You for Your Word. We bless You that we have it in our homes, and that You have given to many of us an understanding and enjoyment of it. Although as yet we do not know what we will know, we have learned from it what we never can forget—that which has changed our lives, has removed our burdens, has comforted our hearts, has set our faces like flints against sin, and has made us eager for perfect holiness.

We thank You, O Lord, for every page of the Book, not only for its promises that are inexpressibly sweet, but also for its precepts in which our souls delight, and especially for the revelation of Your Son, our Lord and Savior Jesus Christ. We thank You for the manifestation of Him in the types and shadows of the Old Testament. These are inexpressibly glorious to us, full of wondrous value, inexpressibly dear, because in them and through them we see the Lord.

But we bless You much more for the clear light of the New Testament, for giving us the key to all the secrets of the Old Testament. Now, as we read the Scriptures of the New Covenant, we understand the language of the Old and are made to joy and to rejoice in it. Father, we thank You for the Book. We thank You for the glorious Man, the God whom the Book reveals as our Savior.

Now we thank You for the blessed Spirit, for without His light upon our understanding, we would have learned nothing. *"The letter killeth, but the spirit giveth life"* (2 Corinthians 3:6). Blessed are our eyes that have been touched with heavenly eye-salve. Blessed are the hearts that have been softened and have been made ready to receive the truth in the love of it! Blessed be the sovereign grace of God, who has chosen unto Him a people who delight in His Word and who meditate on it both day and night!

Our hearts are full of praises to God for this Book of Truth, for this unmeasurable wealth of holy knowledge. Lord, make us enjoy it more and more. May we feed on this manna. May we drink from this well of life. May we be satisfied with it, and by it be conformed to the image of the God from whom it came.

Now, Lord, our prayer to You at the mention of Your sacred Book is that You would write it upon the fleshly tablets of our hearts more fully. We want to know the truth so that the truth may make us free (John 8:32). We want to feel the truth so that we may be sanctified by it. Oh, let it be in us a living seed that will produce in us a life acceptable before God, a life that will be seen in everything that we do unto the living God, for we remember that You are not the God of the dead, but of the living.

Lord, we ask that Your Word may chasten us whenever we go astray. May it enlighten us whenever for a moment we get into darkness. May Your Word be the supreme ruler of our being. May we give ourselves up to its sacred law to be obedient to its every hint, wishing in all things, even in the least things, to do the will of God from the heart and to have every thought brought into captivity to the mind of the Spirit of God (2 Corinthians 10:5).

Bless Your people. Bless them by saturating them with the Word of Your truth. O Lord, they are out in the world so much. Oh, grant that the world may not take them away from their God. Instead, may they get the world under their feet. Do not let them be buried in it, but may they live upon it, treading it beneath their feet. May the spiritual always gain the victory over the material. Oh, that the Word of God might be with us when we are in the midst of an ungodly generation. May the Proverbs furnish us with wisdom, the Psalms comfort us, the Gospels teach us the way of holiness, and the Epistles instruct us in the deep things of the kingdom of God.

Lord, educate us for a higher life, and let that life be begun here. May we always be in school, always be Your disciples. When we are out in the world, may we try to put into practice what we have learned at Jesus' feet. What He tells us in darkness, may we proclaim in the light. What He whispers to us in our prayer closets, may we shout forth from the housetops.

Oh, dear, dear Savior, what could we do without You? We are as yet in banishment. We have not come into the land of light and glory. It is on the other side of the river, in the land where You dwell, the land of Emmanuel. Until we come there, may You be with us. We have said to ourselves, How can we live without our Lord? Then we have said to You, *"If thy presence go not with* [us], *carry us not up hence"* (Exodus 33:15). Oh, be to us this day like the fiery, cloudy pillar that covered all the camp of Israel. May we dwell in God. May we live and move in God. May we be conscious of the presence of God to a far greater extent than we are conscious of anything else.

Bless the churches. Look on them, Lord. Cast an eye of love upon the little companies of the faithful, wherever they may be, and help them and their pastors. In every place may the churches be a light in the midst of this crooked and perverse generation. O God, we are waiting and watching for a display of Your great power among the people.

It is an age of great luxury and great sin and gross departures from the truth. We implore You, defend Your own. When Your ark was carried captive among the Philistines and set up in Dagon's temple, Dagon fell before it (1 Samuel 5:3). Then You *"smote [Your] enemies in the hinder parts: [You] put them to a perpetual reproach"* (Psalm 78:66). You can do the same again, and we pray it may be so. Oh, for the stretched out hand of God! We are longing to see it in the conversion of great multitudes by the Gospel. May those who have said, "Aha, the Gospel has lost its power," be made foolish by the wisdom of the Most High, even as Jannes and Jambres were made foolish when they could not do with their enchantments what God did through His servant.

O Jehovah, You are the true God, God of Abraham, Isaac, and Jacob. You, O God, are our God forever and ever. You will be *"our guide even unto death"* (Psalm 48:14). You who spoke by the apostles speak still by Your servants. Let Your Word have as much power as when You said, *"Let there be light,"* and *"there was light"* (Genesis 1:3). Oh, for the lifting up of Your voice! Let confusion and darkness once again hear the voice of Him who makes order and who gives life. Oh, how we want to stir You up, gracious God. Our prayers would take the form of that ancient one: *"Awake, awake, put* on strength" (Isaiah 51:9). Are You not He who cut Egypt and wounded the crocodile? Do You not still have the same power to smite and to vindicate Your own truth and to deliver Your own redeemed?

O Lamb, slain from before the foundation of the world (Revelation 13:8), You are still sitting upon the throne, for He who is on the throne looks like a Lamb that has been recently slain. O Jesus, we pray, take unto Yourself Your great power. Divide the spoil with the strong. Take the purchase of Your precious blood, and rule *"from the river* [even] *unto the ends of the earth"* (Psalm 72:8).

Here we are before You. Look on us in great pity. Lord, bless Your own people. With favor surround them as with a shield (Psalm 5:12). Lord, save the unsaved. In great compassion draw them by the attractive magnet of the Cross; draw them to Yourself; compel them to come so that the wedding may be furnished with guests.

With one heart we lift up our prayer on the behalf of the teachers of the young. We thank You, Lord, that so many men and women are ready to give their Sabbath's rest to this important service. Oh, grant that zeal for teaching the young may never burn low in the church. May any who are taking no part in it and who ought to be, be aroused at once to begin the holy effort. Bless the teachers of the teenage classes. May their young men and women join the church. May there be no gap between the school and the church. Bridge that distance by Your sovereign grace. But equally bless the teachers of the infants and of the younger children. May conversion go on among the young. May there be multitudes of such conversions. In effect, we pray that no child would leave the Sunday school unsaved. Oh, save the children, great Lover of the little ones. You who allowed them to come to You, You will not forget them, but You will draw them and accept them. Lord, save the children. Let all the classes participate in the blessing that we seek, and by this blessed agency may this nation be kept from heathenism.

May this city especially be preserved from its dogged disregard of the Sabbath, and its carelessness about the things of God. Oh, bless the Sunday schools in every part of London, and let Jesus Christ be glorified among the little ones. May there be heard again loud hosannas in the streets of Jerusalem from the babes and nursing infants, from whose mouths You have ordained strength (Psalm 8:2). Lord, be with the dear workers throughout today and make it a high day, a festival of prayer and faith, a time when Jesus the Lord will especially meet with them and bless them.

God, bless our country! God, save our sovereign! Grant guidance at this time to everyone in regard to the political affairs of this nation. Grant Your blessing to all ranks and every condition of men, and let every nation call You blessed. Let all tongues speak the name of Jesus and all men own Him as Lord and King. We ask it in His name. Amen.

23

God's Unspeakable Gift

O Lord, many of us feel like the lame man at the Beautiful Gate. Come by this way and make the lame ones perfectly sound. O Lord, You can do by Your servants today what You did by them in the olden times. Work miracles of mercy even upon outer-court worshipers who are too lame to get into the Holy Place.

But there are many who feel like that man when he was restored. We want to follow our Restorer, the Prince of Life, into the temple, *"walking, and leaping, and praising God"* (Acts 3:8). He has gone into the temple in the highest sense, up to the throne of God. Made whole, He climbs, and we follow, up the steps of the temple one by one. We come ever nearer to God's throne.

Lord, You have done such great things for us that we feel the drawing of Your love. *"The LORD hath appeared of old unto me, saying, Yea, I have loved thee with an everlasting love: therefore with lovingkindness have I drawn thee"* (Jeremiah 31:3). Draw us, Lord, into the inner sanctuary.

Lord, though healed of a former lameness so that now we have strength, we need a further touch from You. We are so apt to become dull and stupid. Help us, Jesus. A vision of Your face will brighten us, but to feel Your Spirit touching us will make us vigorous. Oh, for the leaping and walking of the man born lame! May we dance with holy joy like David before the ark of the covenant. May a holy elation take possession of every part of us. May our mouths be filled with laughter and our tongues with singing, for *"the Lord hath done great things for us; whereof we are glad"* (Psalm 126:3).

Help Your people to put on Christ. May we live like those who are alive from the dead, for He is the quickening Spirit. Is any part of us still dead? Lord, quicken it. May the life that now possesses our hearts take possession of our heads. May the brain be active in holy thought. May our entire being respond to the life of Christ, and may we live in newness of life.

With pleasure we fall down on our faces and worship the Son of God today. It is such a wonder that He loves us. He has done such wonderful things for us and in us that we may still call Him God's unspeakable gift. He is unspeakably precious to our souls. You know all things, Lord. You know that we love You. May that love bubble up today like a boiling cauldron. May our hearts overflow. If we cannot speak what we feel, may that holy silence be eloquent with the praise of God.

Lord, send Your life throughout the entire church. Visit Your church; restore sound doctrine and holy, earnest living. Take away from professing Christians their love of frivolities, their attempts to meet the world on its own ground, and give back the old love of the doctrines of the Cross and Christ. May free grace and dying love again be the music that refreshes the church and makes her heart exceeding glad.

Lord, wake up dead hearts. If there are seeds of grace lying dormant in any soul, may they begin to bud. May the bulb down at the heart send forth its golden cup and drink in of the light, the life of God. Oh, save today. *"The LORD thy God in the midst of thee is mighty; he will save"* (Zephaniah 3:17). Our very hearts are speaking now much more loudly and sweetly than our lips can speak. Lord, save sinners. Great High Priest, have compassion on the ignorant and those who are not of the way. Great Shepherd of the sheep, gather the lambs within Your arms. Find the lost sheep, throw them on Your shoulders, and bring them home rejoicing.

Lord, with all our hearts we pray for our country. As You bid us, we pray for those in authority, for the sovereign as supreme, for the Parliament, for all magistrates and rulers. We pray also for the poor and the downtrodden.

Lord, look upon the poor and make them rich in faith. Comfort them in heart by the Holy Spirit. Let Your light and Your truth go forth to the most distant parts of the earth. *"Let the people praise thee, O God; let all the people praise thee"* (Psalm 67:3). Give us times of refreshing. May we have a visit from Christ by the power of His Spirit. Until He comes, may there be a blessed time of peace and salvation.

"Thy kingdom come. Thy will be done in earth, as it is in heaven" (Matthew 6:10). And may You come Yourself come, Great King. May our eyes, if it please You, behold You on earth. But if not, if we fall asleep before that blessed day, we can say, *"I know that my redeemer liveth...and though after my skin worms destroy this body, yet in my flesh shall I see God"* (Job 19:25–26).

Bless every Sunday school teacher, every tract distributor, every open-air preacher. Bless, we pray, all nurses, all deacons and missionaries of the City Mission, all Bible readers, and all others who in any way seek to bring men to Christ. O God, flood the world with a baptism of Your power, and let the whole earth *"be filled with the knowledge of the glory of the LORD, as the waters cover the sea"* (Habakkuk 2:14).

We ask all in that dear name that made the lame man whole, the name that is sweet to God in heaven and dear to us below. Unto Father, Son, and Holy Spirit be glory forever. Amen.

24

"Deliver Us from Evil"

God, do not let us be formalists or hypocrites during this time of prayer. We feel how easy it is to bow our heads and cover our faces, and yet our thoughts may be all astray; our minds may be wandering hither and yon, so that there can be no real prayer at all. Come, Holy Spirit; help us feel that we are in the immediate presence of God. May this thought lead us to sincere, earnest petitioning.

There are some who do not know You, God. You are not in their thoughts. They make no acknowledgment of You, glorious One, but do their business and guide their lives as if there were no God in heaven or in earth. Strike them now with a sense of Your presence. May Your eternal power come before their thoughts, and now may they join Your reverent people in approaching Your mercy seat.

We come for mercy, great God. It must always be our first request, for we have sinned against a just and holy law of which our consciences approve. We are evil, but Your law is holy and just and good. We have offended knowingly. We have offended again and again. After being chastened, we have still offended. Even we who are forgiven, who through Your rich love have been once for all washed from every stain, sin grievously. We confess it with much shame and bitter self-reproach that we sin against such tender love and against the indwelling Holy Spirit, who is in His people and who checks us and quickens our consciences, so that we sin against light and knowledge when we sin.

Wash us yet again. When we ask for this washing, it is not because we doubt the efficacy of former cleansing. Then we were washed in blood. Now, O Savior, repeat with us what You did to the Twelve when You took a towel and basin and washed their feet. You told them that he who had been washed had no need except to wash his feet. After that was done, he was *"clean every whit"* (John 13:10). Oh, let Your children be in that condition now—*"clean every whit"*—and may we know it. Thus being clean, may we have boldness to enter into the Holy of Holies by the blood of Christ. May we now come and stand where the cherubim were, where the glory still shines forth. There before a blood-sprinkled mercy seat, washed and cleansed, may we pour out our prayers and praises.

As for those who never have been washed, we repeat our prayer for them. Bring them, O Lord, bring them at once to a deep sense of sin and to the complete realization of Your unmerited grace through the shed blood of Your Son. May we see them take their first complete washing. From now on, may they become the blood-washed and blood-redeemed consecrated ones, belonging forever to Him who has made them white through His atoning sacrifice.

Blessed Lord, since You do permit Your washed ones to come close to You, we want to approach You now with the courage that comes from faith and love and ask of You this thing: help us to overcome every tendency to evil that is still within us, and enable us to wear armor of such strength that the arrows of the enemy from without may not penetrate it, that we may not be wounded again by sin. Deliver us, we pray, from doubts within and fears without, from depression of spirit, and from the outward assaults of the world. Make us and keep us pure within, and then let our lives be conducted with such holy vigilance and watchfulness that there may be nothing about us that would bring dishonor to Your name. May those who most carefully watch us see nothing but what would adorn the doctrine of God our Savior in all things.

Lord, help Your people to be right as parents. May none of us spoil our children. May there be no poorly managed families to cry out against us. Help us to be right as employers. May there be no oppression, no hardness, and no unkindness. Help us to be right as employees. May there be no slipshod service, no pilfering, but may there be everything that adorns the Christian character. Keep us right as citizens. May we do all we can for our country and for the times in which we live. Keep us right, we pray, as citizens of the higher country. May we be living for it, to enjoy its privileges and to bring others within its borders, that multitudes may be made citizens of Christ through our means.

Lord, help us to conduct ourselves fittingly as church members. May we love our brothers and sisters. May we seek their good, their edification, their comfort, their health. May those of us who are called to preach have grace equal to that responsibility. Lord, make every Christian be aware of the blood of all those around him. We know that there are some who profess to be Your people who do not seem to care one bit about the souls of their fellowmen. God forgive this inhumanity to men, this treason to the King of Kings. Rouse the church, we pray, to a tenderness of heart toward those among whom we dwell.

Let all the churches feel that they are ordained to bless their neighbors. Oh, that the Christian church in England might begin to take upon itself its true burden. Let the church in London especially, with its mass of poverty and sin around it, care for and love the people. May all Christians rouse themselves to do something for the good of men and for the glory of God. Lord, use us for Your glory.

Shine upon us, O Emmanuel. May we reflect Your brightness. Dwell in us, O Jesus, that out of us may come the power of Your life. Cause Your church to work miracles, because the Miracle Worker is in the midst of her. Oh, send us times of revival, seasons of great refreshing, and then times of aggression when the army of the Lord of Hosts will push its way into the very center of the adversary and overthrow the foe in the name of the King of Kings.

Now forgive Your servants all that has been amiss, and strengthen in Your servants all that is good and right. Sanctify us to Your service, and hold us to it. Comfort us with Your presence. Elevate us into Your presence. Make us like You. In all things glorify Yourself in us, whether we live or die.

O Lord, bless the poor. Remember the needy among Your own people. Help and relieve them. Bless the sick, and be very near the dying. May the Lord comfort them.

Bless our country. Let every mercy rest upon those in government. Send peace to disquieted districts. Give wisdom to our senators in making and in attending to the keeping of the law. And may Your kingdom come not here only, but in every land and nation. Remember

with the plenitude of Your grace lands across
the sea. Let the whole earth be filled with Your
glory. We ask it for Jesus' sake. Amen.

25

"The Washing of Water by the Word"

Lord, our God, You love Your people; You have placed all the saints in the hand of Jesus; and You have given Jesus to be their leader, commander, and husband. We know that You delight to hear us cry on the behalf of Your church, for You care for her, and You are ready to grant to her according to the covenant provisions that You have laid up in store for Christ Jesus. Therefore, we begin this prayer by entreating You to behold and visit the vine and the vineyard that Your right hand has planted. *"Look upon Zion, the city of our solemnities"* (Isaiah 33:20). Look upon those whom You have chosen from before the foundation of the world, whom Christ has redeemed with blood, whose hearts He has won and holds, and who are His although they are in the world.

Holy Father, keep Your people, we pray, for Jesus' sake. Though they are in the world, do not let them be of it, but may there be a marked distinction between them and the rest of mankind. Even as their Lord was holy, harmless, undefiled, and separate from sinners, so may it be with believers in Christ. May they follow Him. May they not know the voice of strangers but come out from the rest so that they may follow Him outside the camp (Hebrews 13:13).

We cry to You for the preservation of Your church in the world, and especially for her purity. Oh, Father, keep us, we implore You, with all keeping, so that the evil one does not touch us. We will be tempted, but do not let him prevail against us. In a thousand ways he will lay snares for our feet, but deliver us *as a bird out of the snare of the fowlers* (Psalm 124:7). May the snare be broken so that we may escape. Do not let Your church suffer dishonor at any time, but may her garments always be white. Do not let those who come in among her who are not of her utterly despoil her. O Christ, as You groaned concerning Judas, so may Your children cry to You concerning any who have fallen aside into crooked ways, lest the cause of Christ in the earth should be dishonored. O God, cover, we pray, all the people of Christ with Your feathers (Psalm 91:4). Keep the church even until Christ returns, who, having loved His own who were in the world, loves them even to the end (John 13:1).

We want to ask just now that our feet may be washed. We trust You have bathed us once for all in the sin-removing fountain. You have also washed us in the waters of regeneration and given us the renewing of our minds through Jesus Christ. But now we cry for daily cleansing! Do You see any fault in us? We know that You do. Wash us so that we may be clean. Are we deficient in any virtue? Oh, supply it so that we may exhibit a perfect character to the glory of Him who has made us anew in Christ Jesus. Or is there something that would be good if not carried to excess? Be pleased to modify it, lest one virtue would overpower another, and we would not be the image of Christ completely.

O Lord and Master, You who washed Your disciples' feet of old, still be very patient toward us, very gracious toward our provoking faults, and go on with us, we pray, until Your great work is completed and we are brothers of the First Born, like unto Him. Gracious Master, we wish to conquer self in every respect. We desire to live for the glory of God and the good of our fellowmen. May You enable us especially to overcome the body with all its affections and lusts. May the flesh be kept under submission. Let no appetite of any kind of the grosser sort prevail against our personhood, lest we be dishonored and unclean. Do not let even the most refined power of the natural mind be permitted to come forward if in any way it would mar the dominion of the Spirit of God within us.

Oh, help us not to be so easily moved even by pain. May we have much patience. Do not let the prospect of death ever cause us any fear, but may the spirit so get the mastery of the body that we know nothing can hurt the true man. The inner newborn man cannot be smitten, nor is it to die. It is holy, incorruptible, and lives and abides forever in the life that is in Christ Jesus.

Oh, for a complete conquest of self! Render us unaffected by praise, we pray, lest we be too sensitive to censure. Let us believe that to have the approval of God and of our own consciences is quite enough. May we be content, gracious God, to bear the faultfinding of unreasonable men and the misrepresentations of our own brothers. If those whom we love do not love us, may we love them nevertheless. If they misjudge us by mistake, let us have no hard feelings toward them. God, grant that we may never misjudge one another. Does not our Judge stand in the courtroom? Oh, keep us like little children who do not know, but expect to know hereafter, and are content to believe things that they do not understand. Lord, keep us humble, dependent, yet serenely joyful. May we be calm and quiet even as a weaned child, yet may we be earnest and active.

O Savior, make us like Yourself. We do not wish so much to do as to be. If You will make us to be right, we will do right. We find how often we have to put a constraint upon ourselves to be right. Oh, that we were like You, Jesus, so that we had only to be ourselves, to behave in our perfect holiness! We will never rest until this is the case, until You have made us inwardly holy. Then words and actions must be holy as a matter of course. Now, here we are, Lord, and we belong to You. Oh, it is because we are Your own that we have hope. You will make us worthy of You. Your possession of us is our hope of perfection. You wash our feet because we are Your own. How sweet is the mercy that first took us to its heart and made us all its own and now continues to deal tenderly with us! Being Christ's own, may we have that of Christ within us that all may see and that proves us to be Christ's own!

We bring before You all Your saints and ask You to attend to their trials and troubles. Some we know are afflicted personally, others in their dear friends and families, and some in their temporal state, having been brought into sore distress. Lord, we do not know the trials of all Your people, but You do, for You are the Head, and the pains of all the members are centered in You. Help Your people.

Now we pray that You would grant us the blessing that we have already sought, and let it come upon all the churches of our beloved country. May the Lord revive true and undefiled religion here and in all the other lands where Christ is known and preached. Let the day come when heathendom becomes converted, when the crescent of Mohammed wanes into eternal night, and when she who sits on the Seven Hills and exalts herself in the place of God is cast down to sink like a millstone in the flood.

Let the blessed Gospel of the eternal God prevail. *"Let the whole earth be filled with his glory"* (Psalm 72:19). Oh, that we may live to see that day. Lord, bless our country. Have pity on it. God, bless those in government with every mercy and blessing. Oh, let the people see Your hand and understand why it is laid upon them, so that they may turn from wrongdoing and seek righteousness and follow after peace. Then will the blessing return. May You hear us as we often cry to You in secret on behalf of this misled land. Lord, deliver it, and lift up the light of Your countenance upon it yet again, for Jesus' sake. Amen.

26

Prayer Answered and Unanswered

God of Israel, our Lord and King forever and ever! Help us now by the sacred Spirit to approach You appropriately with deepest reverence, but not with servile fear; with holiest boldness, but not with presumption. Teach us as children to speak to the Father, and yet as creatures to bow before our Maker.

Our Father, we want to first ask You whether You have anything against us as Your children. Have we been asking of You amiss, and have You given us what we have sought? We are not conscious of it, but it may be so. Now we are brought as an answer to our presumptuous prayers into a more difficult position than the one we occupied before. Now it may be that some creature comfort is nearer to us than our God. We would have been better off without it and to have dwelt in our God and there to have found our joy. But now, Lord, in these perilous circumstances, give us grace so that we may not turn away from You.

If our position is not such as You would have allotted to us had we been wiser, nevertheless grant that we may be taught to behave ourselves appropriately even now, lest the mercies You have given should become a cause of stumbling and the obtaining of our hearts' desires should become a temptation to us.

Rather, we feel inclined to bless You for the many occasions in which You have not answered our prayers, for You have said that we did ask amiss and therefore we could not have (James 4:3). We desire to register this prayer with You—that whenever we do ask amiss, You would in great wisdom and love be pleased to refuse us.

O Lord, if we at any time press our suit without sufficient resignation, do not regard us, we pray. Though we cry to You day and night concerning anything, if You see that we err, do not regard the voice of our cry, we ask You. It is our hearts' desire now, in our cooler moments, that this prayer of ours might stand on record as long as we live: *"Nevertheless not my will, but thine, be done"* (Luke 22:42).

O Lord, in looking back, we are obliged to remember with the greatest gratitude the many occasions in which You have heard our cries. When we have been brought into deep distress and our hearts have sunk within us, then we have cried to You, and You have never refused to hear us. The prayers of our lusts You have rejected, but the prayers of our necessities You have granted. Not one good thing has failed of all that You have promised.

You have given to us exceedingly abundantly above what we asked or even thought, for there was a day when our present condition would have been regarded as much too high for us ever to reach. In looking back, we are surprised that those who lay among the pots of Egypt should now sit every man under his vine and fig tree, that those who wandered in the wilderness in a solitary way should now find a city to dwell in, that we who were prodigals in rags should now be children in the Father's house, and that we who were companions of swine should now be made heirs of God and joint-heirs with Christ. What encouragement we have to pray to such a prayer-hearing God, who far exceeds the requests of His children.

"Blessed be the name of the Lord forever," our innermost hearts are saying. "Amen, blessed be His name!" If it were only for answered prayer or even for some unanswered prayers, we would continue to praise and bless You as long as we have any being (Psalm 104:33).

Now, Lord, listen to the voice of Your children's cry. Wherever there is a sincere heart seeking for greater holiness, may You answer that request. Wherever there is a broken spirit seeking reconciliation with You, be pleased to answer it now. You know where there is prayer, though it is unuttered, and even the lips do not move. Oh, hear the publican who dares not lift his eye to heaven. Hear him when he cries, *"God be merciful to me a sinner"* (Luke 18:13). Hear those who seem to themselves to be appointed unto death. Let the sighing of the prisoner come before You! Oh, that You would grant peace and rest to every troubled spirit all over the world who now desires to turn his face to the Cross and to see God in Christ Jesus.

O Lord, if there are any of Your servants concerned about the cares of others, we thank You for them. Raise up in the church many intercessors who would plead for the prosperity of Zion and give You no rest until You establish her and make her a joy in the land.

Oh, there are some of us who have cried to You about our country. You know how in secret we have groaned and sighed over evil times. You have begun to hear us already, for which we desire to praise and bless Your name. But we do not cease to pray for this land that You would roll away from it all its sin, that You would deliver it from the curse of drunkenness, rescue it from unbelief, ritualism, rationalism, and every form of evil, so that this land might become a holy land.

O Lord, bring the multitudes of workingmen to listen to the Gospel. Break in, we pray, upon their stolid indifference. Lord, give them a love of Your house, a desire to hear Your Gospel. Then may You look upon the poor rich, so many of whom know nothing about You and are worshiping their own wealth. Lord, grant that the many for whom there are no special gospel services, but who are wrapped up in self-righteousness, be brought to hear the Gospel of Jesus so that they also may be brought to Christ. God, bless this land with more gospel light, gospel life, and gospel love. You will hear us, O Lord.

Then we want to pray for our children, that they might be saved. Some of us no longer need to pray for our children's conversions, for our prayers have been heard already. But there are others who have children who worry them and grieve their hearts. O God, save sons and daughters of godly people. Do not let them have to sigh over their children as Eli and Samuel did. May they see their sons and daughters become children of the living God. We want to pray for our coworkers, for our neighbors, for our relatives of near or far degree, that all might be brought to Jesus. Do this, O God, in Your infinite mercy.

As we are now making intercession, we want to pray according to Your Word for all kings and for all who are in authority, so that we may lead quiet and peaceable lives (1 Timothy 2:1–2). We pray for all nations also. O Lord, bless and remember the lands that sit in darkness, and let them see a great light. May

missionary endeavors be abundantly success-
ful. Let the favored nations where our God is
known, especially this land and the land
across the mighty ocean, which love the same
Savior and speak the same language, be always favored with the divine presence and with
abundant prosperity and blessing.

And now, Father, glorify Your Son! In
scattering pardons through His precious blood,
glorify Your Son! In sending forth the Eternal
Spirit to convict men and bring them to His
feet, Father, glorify Your Son! In enriching
Your saints with gifts and graces and building
them up into His image, Father, glorify Your
Son! In the gathering together of the whole
company of His elect and in the hastening of
His kingdom and His coming, Father, glorify
Your Son! Beyond this prayer we cannot go:
*"Glorify thy Son, that thy Son also may glorify
thee"* (John 17:1). Unto Father, Son, and Holy
Spirit be glory forever and ever. Amen.

Epilogue:
The Golden Key of Prayer

Call unto me, and I will answer thee,
and show thee great and mighty things,
which thou knowest not.
—Jeremiah 33:3

Some of the most learned works in the world smell of the midnight oil, but the most spiritual and most comforting books and sayings of men usually have an aroma about them of damp prison. I could cite many instances, but John Bunyan's *Pilgrim's Progress* may suffice instead of a hundred others. And this good Scripture text of ours, all moldy and chilled with the prison in which Jeremiah lay, has nevertheless a brightness and a beauty about it that it might never have had if it had not come as a cheering word to the prisoner of the Lord, who was shut up in the court of the prison house.

God's people have always, when in the worst of conditions, found out the best of their

God. He is good at all times, but He seems to
be at His best when they are at their worst.
"How could you bear your long imprisonment
so well?" said one to the Landgrave of Hesse,
who had been locked up for his attachment to
the principles of the Reformation. He replied,
"The divine consolations of martyrs were with
me." Doubtless there is a consolation deeper
and stronger than any other, which God keeps
for those who, being His faithful witnesses,
have to endure exceedingly great tribulation
from the enmity of man.

There is a glorious aurora for the frigid
zone, and stars glisten in Northern skies with
unusual splendor. The Scottish preacher
Samuel Rutherford had a quaint saying, that
when he was cast into the cellars of affliction,
he remembered that the Great King always
kept His wine there. He began to seek at once
for the wine bottles and to drink of the well-
refined wine.

They who dive in the sea of affliction bring
up rare pearls. You know, my companions in
affliction, that it is so. You whose bones have
been ready to come through your skin because
of lying long upon the weary couch, you who
have seen your earthly goods carried away
from you and have been reduced nearly to
poverty, you who have gone to the graveside
even seven times until you have feared that
your last earthly friend would be borne away
by unpitying death, you have proved that He is

a faithful God and that, as your tribulations abound, so your consolations also abound by Christ Jesus (2 Corinthians 1:5). My prayer is that some other prisoners of the Lord may have this text's joyous promise spoken inwardly to them. I pray that you who are tightly shut away and cannot come forth because of a present heaviness of spirit may hear Him say, as with a soft whisper in your ears and in your hearts, *"Call unto me, and I will answer thee, and show thee great and mighty things, which thou knowest not."*

The text naturally divides itself into three distinct truths. I will explain these as I am enabled by God the Holy Spirit. First, prayer is commanded: *"Call unto me."* Second, an answer is promised: *"And I will answer thee."* Third, faith is encouraged: *"And show thee great and mighty things, which thou knowest not."*

GOD'S COMMAND TO PRAY

The first truth of this Scripture is that prayer is commanded. We are not merely counseled and recommended to pray, but commanded to pray. This is tremendous graciousness on God's part. If a hospital is built and free admission is given to the sick when they seek it, no order is made that a man *must* enter its gates. A soup kitchen may be well-stocked for the depths of winter, and notice may be circulated that those who are poor may receive food upon application, but no one thinks of passing a law compelling the poor to come and wait in line to take the charity. It is thought to be enough to offer it without issuing a mandate that men *must* accept it. Yet so strange is man's mentality on the one hand that it makes him need a command to be merciful to his own soul, and so marvelous is the condescension of our gracious God on the other that He issues a command of love, without which not one man born of Adam would partake of the gospel feast, but would rather starve than come.

Worldly Distractions

It is true even in the matter of prayer. God's own people need a command to pray, or else they would not receive it. How is this? Because, friends, we are very subject to fits of worldliness, if indeed that is not our usual state. We do not forget to eat or to go to our beds to rest. We do not forget to be diligent in business. Yet we often forget to wrestle with God in prayer and to spend, as we ought to spend, long periods in consecrated fellowship with our Father and our God.

With too many professing believers, the worldly ledger is so bulky that you cannot move it, and the Bible, representing their devotion, is so small that you could almost put it in your pocket. Hours for the world! Moments for Christ! The world has the best of our time, and our prayer closets the leftover fragments. We give our strength and freshness to the ways of money, and our weakness and fatigue to the ways of God. This is why we need to be commanded to attend to that very act that ought to be our greatest happiness, as it is our highest privilege to perform—to meet with Him. *"Call unto me,"* He says, for He knows that we are apt to forget to call upon Him. *"What meanest thou, O sleeper? arise, call upon thy God"* (Jonah 1:6) is an exhortation that is needed by us as well as it was needed by Jonah in the storm.

Burdened Hearts

He understands what heavy hearts we have sometimes, when we are under a sense of sin. Satan says to us, "Why should you pray? How can you hope to prevail? In vain you say, *'I will arise and go to my father'* (Luke 15:18), for you are not worthy to be one of his hired servants. How can you see the King's face after you have played the traitor against Him? How will you dare to approach the altar when you have yourself defiled it and when the sacrifice that you would bring is a poor, polluted one?"

Beloved, it is well for us that we are commanded to pray, or else in times of heaviness we might not. If God commands me, unfit as I may be, I will creep to the footstool of grace.

Since He says, *"Pray without ceasing"* (1 Thessalonians 5:17), though my words fail me and my heart itself wanders, I will stammer out the wishes of my thirsty soul and say, "O God, teach me to pray, and help me to prevail with You."

Frequent Unbelief

Are we not commanded to pray also because of our frequent unbelief? Unbelief whispers, "What profit is there if you do seek the Lord about that matter?" The foul fiend of hell suggests to you, "This is a case quite out of the bounds of those things in which God has intervened. Therefore, if you were in any other position, you might rest upon the mighty arm of God, but here your prayer will not help you. It is too trivial a matter. It is too connected with temporal things. It is a matter in which you have sinned too much. It is too high, too hard, too complicated a piece of business. You have no right to take that before God!" So the Devil continues.

Therefore, there stands written as an everyday precept, suitable to every case into which a Christian can be cast, *"'Call unto me.'* Are you sick? Do you want to be healed? Cry unto Me, for I am a Great Physician. Does providence trouble you? Are you fearful that you will not respect what is right in the sight of man? *'Call unto me!'* Do Your children trouble you? Do you feel that which is sharper than an adder's tooth—a thankless child? *'Call unto me.'* Are your griefs little, yet painful, like small points and pricks of thorns? *'Call unto me!'* Is your burden so heavy it would make your back break beneath its load? *'Call unto me!'"*

"Cast thy burden upon the LORD, and he shall sustain thee: he shall never suffer the righteous to be moved" (Psalm 55:22). In the valley; on the mountain; on the barren rock; in the briny sea, submerged beneath the billows, and lifted up by and by upon the crest of the waves; in the furnace when the coals are glowing; in the gates of death when the jaws of hell would shut themselves upon you—cease not, for the commandment ever says to you, *"Call unto me."* Prayer is still mighty and must prevail with God to bring you your deliverance. These are some of the reasons that the privilege of supplication is also spoken of as a duty in Holy Scripture. There are many more, but these will suffice for now.

A Sure and Abiding Command

Also, we ought to be very glad that God has given us this command in His Word that it may be sure and abiding. You may turn to fifty passages where the same precept is uttered. I do not often read in Scripture, *"Thou shalt not kill....Thou shalt not covet"* (Exodus 20:13, 17). Twice the law is given, but I often read gospel precepts. If the law is given twice, the Gospel is given seventy times seven. For every precept that I cannot keep by reason of my being weak through the flesh, I find a thousand precepts that are sweet and pleasant for me to keep by reason of the power of the Holy Spirit that dwells in all children of God. This command to pray is insisted upon repeatedly.

It may be a revealing exercise for some of you to find out how often in Scripture you are told to pray. You will be surprised to find how many times such words as these are given: *"Call upon me in the day of trouble: I will deliver thee"* (Psalm 50:15). *"Ye people, pour out your heart before him"* (Psalm 62:8). *"Seek ye the LORD while he may be found, call ye upon him while he is near"* (Isaiah 55:6). *"Ask, and it shall be given you; seek, and ye shall find; knock, and it shall be opened unto you"* (Matthew 7:7). *"Watch ye and pray, lest ye enter into temptation"* (Mark 14:38). *"Pray without ceasing"* (1 Thessalonians 5:17). *"Come boldly unto the throne of grace"* (Hebrews 4:16). *"Draw nigh to God, and he will draw nigh to you"* (James 4:8). *"Continue in prayer"* (Colossians 4:2). I do not need to multiply what I could not possibly exhaust. I have picked eight or nine out of this great bag of pearls.

Our Right to Pray

Come, Christian, you should never question whether you have a right to pray. You should never ask, "May I be permitted to come into His presence?" When you have so many commands (and God's commands are all promises and all enablings), you may come boldly unto the throne of heavenly grace, by the new and living way through the rent veil.

The Urging of the Holy Spirit

But there are times when not only does God command His people to pray through the Bible, but He also directly commands them to pray by the urging of His Holy Spirit. You who know the inner life understand what I am saying. You feel all of a sudden, possibly in the midst of business, the pressing thought that you *must* get alone and pray. It may be that you do not take particular notice of the inclination at first, but it comes again and again: "Get alone and pray!"

I find that in the matter of prayer, I am myself very much like a waterwheel, which runs well when there is plenty of water but turns with very little force when the brook is growing shallow. I could also be likened to a ship that flies over the waves and puts out all her canvas when the wind is favorable, but has to tack about most laboriously when there is only a little of the favoring breeze.

Now, it strikes me that whenever our Lord gives you the special inclination to pray, you should double your diligence. *"Men ought always to pray, and not to faint"* (Luke 18:1). Yet when He gives you the special longing to pray and you feel a special enjoyment in it, you have, over and above the command that is constantly binding, another command that should compel you to cheerful obedience. At such times, I think we may stand in the position of David, to whom the Lord said, *"When thou hearest the sound of a going* [marching] *in the tops of the mulberry trees...then thou shalt bestir thyself"* (2 Samuel 5:24). That *"going in the tops of the mulberry trees"* may have been the footsteps of angels hastening to help David. Then David was to smite the Philistines.

When God's mercies are approaching, their footsteps are our desires to pray. Our desires to pray should be at once an indication that His time to favor Zion is coming. Sow plentifully now, for you can sow in hope. Plow joyously now, for your harvest is sure. Wrestle now, Jacob, for you are about to be made a prevailing prince, and your name will be called Israel. Now is your time, spiritual merchants: the market is high; trade much. Your profit will be large. See to it that you use the golden hour well, and reap your harvest while the sun shines.

When we enjoy visitations from on high, we should be particularly constant in prayer. If some other less-pressing duty must be set aside for a season, it will not go amiss, and we will not lose out. When God specially bids us to pray by the urgings of His Spirit, then we should stir ourselves in prayer.

GOD'S ANSWERS TO PRAYER

God's Nature

Now let us look at the second point: an answer is promised. We should not tolerate for even a moment the ghastly and grievous thought that God will not answer prayer. His nature, as manifested in Christ Jesus, demands the answer. He has revealed Himself in the Gospel as a God of love, *"full of grace and truth"* (John 1:14). How can He refuse to help those of His creatures who humbly in His own appointed way seek His face and favor?

On one occasion, the Athenian senate found it convenient to meet together in the open air. As they were sitting in their deliberations, a sparrow, pursued by a hawk, flew in the direction of the senate. Being hard-pressed by the bird of prey, it sought shelter in the coat of one of the senators. He, being a man of rough and vulgar mold, took the bird from his coat, threw it to the ground, and so killed it. Whereupon the whole senate rose in an uproar and, without a single dissenting voice, condemned him to die. They judged him unworthy of a seat in the senate with them or to be called an Athenian, since he did not give help to a creature that confided in him.

Can we suppose that the God of heaven, whose nature is love, could tear out of His garment the poor fluttering dove that flies from the eagle of justice into the garment of His mercy? Will He give the invitation to us to seek His face, and when we, with much trepidation and fear, do summon courage enough to fly to Him, will He then be unjust and ungracious enough to forget to hear our cry and to answer us? Let us not think so harshly of the God of heaven.

God's Past Character

Let us recollect next His past character as well as His nature. I mean the character that He has won for Himself by His past deeds of grace. Consider, beloved, the one stupendous display of bounty: *"He...spared not his own Son, but delivered him up for us all"* (Romans 8:32). If I were to mention a thousand illustrations, I could not give a better picture of the character of God than that one deed. However, not only my inference, but the inspired conclusion of the apostle is, *"How shall he not with him also freely give us all things?"* (v. 32).

If the Lord did not refuse to listen to my voice when I was a guilty sinner and an enemy, how can He disregard my cry now that I am justified and saved? How is it that He heard the voice of my misery when my heart did not hear it and would not seek relief, if after all He will not hear me now that I am His child and His friend? The bleeding wounds of Jesus are the sure guarantees for answered prayer. George

Herbert in that quaint poem of his, *The Bag,* represents the Savior as saying,

> If ye have anything to send or write
>   (I have no bag, but here is room)
> Unto My Father's hands and sight,
>   (Believe Me) it shall safely come.
> That I shall mind what you impart
>   Look, you may put it very near My heart,
> Or if hereafter any of friends
>   Will use Me in this kind, the door
> Shall still be open; what he sends
>   I will present and somewhat more
>   Not to his hurt.

Surely, George Herbert's thoughts were that the Atonement was in itself a guarantee that prayer must be heard, and that the great gash made near the Savior's heart, which let light into the very depths of the heart of Deity, was proof that He who sits in heaven would hear the cry of His people. You misread Calvary if you think that prayer is useless.

God's Own Promise

But, beloved, we also have the Lord's own promise for it, and He is a God who cannot lie. *"Call upon me in the day of trouble: I will deliver thee"* (Psalm 50:15). Has He not said, *"Whatsoever ye shall ask in prayer, believing, ye shall receive"* (Matthew 21:22)? We cannot pray, indeed, unless we believe this doctrine: *"For he that cometh to God must believe that he is, and that he is a rewarder of them that diligently seek him"* (Hebrews 11:6). If we have any question at all about whether our prayer will be heard, we are comparable to him who wavers: *"But let him ask in faith, nothing wavering. For he that wavereth is like a wave of the sea driven with the wind and tossed. For let not that man think that he shall receive any thing of the Lord"* (James 1:6–7).

Our Own Experiences

Furthermore, it is not necessary, but it may strengthen the point to add that our own experiences lead us to believe that God will answer prayer. I must not speak for you, but I may speak for myself. If there is anything I know, anything that I am quite assured of beyond all question, it is that praying breath is never spent in vain. If no other human being can say it, I dare to say it, and I know that I can prove it. My own conversion is the result of long, affectionate, earnest, unrelenting prayer. My parents prayed for me, God heard their cries, and here I am to preach the Gospel. Since then I have ventured on some things that were far beyond my mere capacity, but I have never failed because I have cast myself upon the Lord. You know as a church that I have not hesitated to indulge large ideas of what we might do for God, and we have accomplished all that we purposed. I have sought God's aid, assistance, and help in all my many undertakings. Though I cannot tell here the story of my private life in God's work, yet if it were written, it would be a standing proof that there is a God who answers prayer.

God has heard my prayers, not now and then, not once or twice, but so many times that it has grown into a habit with me to spread my case before God with the absolute certainty that whatsoever I ask of God, He will give to me. It is not just a "perhaps" or a "maybe." I know that my Lord answers me, and I dare not doubt. It would be foolishness if I did.

As I am sure that a certain amount of leverage will lift a weight, so I know that a certain amount of prayer will get anything from God. As the rain cloud brings the shower, so prayer brings the blessing. As spring scatters flowers, so supplication ensures mercies. In all labor there is profit, but most of all in the work of intercession I am sure of this, for I have reaped it. As I put trust in our currency and have never failed yet to buy what I want when I produce the cash, so I put trust in God's promises. I intend to do so until I find that He tells me that they are worthless coins and will not do as trade in heaven's market. But why should I speak? Oh, beloved, you all know in your own selves that God hears prayer. If you do not, then where is your Christianity? Where is your belief? You will need to learn the first elements of the truth, for all saints, young or old, count it certain that He hears prayer.

Submission to God's Will

Still remember that prayer is always to be offered in submission to God's will. When we say that God hears prayer, we do not mean that He always gives us literally what we ask for. However, we do mean this: that He gives us what is best for us, and that if He does not give us the mercy we ask for in silver, He bestows it upon us in gold. If He does not take away the thorn in the flesh, yet He says, *"My grace is sufficient for thee"* (2 Corinthians 12:9), which amounts to the same in the end.

Lord Bolingbroke said to the Countess of Huntingdon, who founded a body of Calvinistic Methodists, "I cannot understand, Your Ladyship, how you can make earnest prayer to be consistent with submission to the divine will." "My lord," she replied, "that is a matter of no difficulty. If I were a courtier of some generous king, and he gave me permission to ask any favor I pleased of him, I would be sure to put it this way, 'Will Your Majesty be graciously pleased to grant me such and such a favor? But at the same time, though I very much desire it, if it would in any way detract from Your Majesty's honor, or if in Your Majesty's judgment it seems better that I do not have this favor, I will be just as content to go without it as to receive it.' So you see, I might earnestly offer a petition, and yet I might submissively leave it in the king's hands."

So it is with God. We never offer prayer without inserting that clause, either in spirit or in words, *"Nevertheless not as I will, but as thou wilt"* (Matthew 26:39). *"Not my will, but thine, be done"* (Luke 22:42). We can only pray without an "if" when we are quite sure that our will is God's will because God's will is fully our will. A much slandered poet has well said,

> Man, regard thy prayers as a purpose of
>   love to thy soul,
> Esteem the providence that led to them as
>   an index of God's good will;
> So shalt thou pray aright, and thy words
>   shall meet with acceptance.
> Also, in pleading for others, be thankful for
>   the fullness of thy prayer;
> For if thou art ready to ask, the Lord is
>   more ready to bestow.
> The salt preserveth the sea, and the saints
>   uphold the earth;
> Their prayers are the thousand pillars that
>   prop the canopy of nature.
> Verily, an hour without prayer, from some
>   terrestrial mind,
> Were a curse in the calendar of time, a spot
>   of the blackness of darkness.
> Perchance the terrible day, when the world
>   must rock into ruins,
> Will be one unwhitened by prayer—shall He
>   find faith on the earth?

For there is an economy of mercy, as of wisdom,
    and power, and means;
Neither is one blessing granted, unbesought
    from the treasury of good:
And the charitable heart of the Being, to
    depend upon whom is happiness,
Never withholdeth a bounty, so long as His
    subject prayeth;
Yea, ask what thou wilt, to the second
    throne in heaven,
It is thine for whom it was appointed; there
    is no limit unto prayer:
But and if thou cease to ask, tremble, thou
    self-suspended creature,
For thy strength is cut off as was Samson's:
    and the hour of thy doom is come.

ENCOURAGEMENT TO BELIEVE GOD

I come to our third truth, which I think is full of assurance to all those who exercise the hallowed art of prayer: faith is encouraged. *"I will...show thee great and mighty things, which thou knowest not."*

This word was originally spoken to a prophet in prison. Therefore, in the first place, it applies to every teacher. Indeed, since every teacher must be a learner, it also has a bearing upon every learner of divine truth. The best way by which a prophet, teacher, or learner can know the reserved truths, the higher and more mysterious truths of God, is by waiting upon God in prayer.

Prayer Promotes Learning

I especially noticed in reading the book of Daniel, how Daniel found out Nebuchadnez-zar's dream. The soothsayers, magicians, and astrologers of the Chaldees brought out their curious books and strange instruments, and began to mutter *abracadabra* and all sorts of mysterious incantations, but they failed. What did Daniel do? He set himself to pray. Knowing that the prayer of a united body of people has more prevailing power than the prayer of one, Daniel called together his compatriots and told them to unite with him in earnest prayer that God would be pleased in His infinite mercy to open up the vision.

> *Then Daniel went to his house, and made the thing known to Hananiah, Mishael, and Azariah, his companions: that they would desire mercies of the God of heaven concerning this secret; that Daniel and his fellows should not perish with the rest of the wise men of Babylon. Then was the secret revealed unto Daniel in a night vision. Then Daniel blessed the God of heaven.*
> (Daniel 2:17–19)

In the case of John, who was the Daniel of the New Testament, you remember he saw a book in the right hand of Him who sat on the throne—a book sealed with seven seals that none was found worthy to open or to look

179

upon. What did John do? The book was eventually opened by the Lion of the tribe of Judah, who had prevailed to open the book. But it is written first, before the book was opened, *"I wept much"* (Revelation 5:4). Yes, the tears of John, which were his liquid prayers, were, as far as he was concerned, the sacred keys by which the book was opened.

Pastors in the ministry, Sunday school teachers, and all of you who are learners in the college of Christ Jesus, remember that prayer is your best means of study. Like Daniel, you will understand the dream and its interpretation when you have sought God. Like John, you will see the seven seals of precious truth unloosed after you have wept much.

> *Yea, if thou criest after knowledge, and liftest up thy voice for understanding; if thou seekest her as silver, and searchest for her as for hid treasures; then shalt thou understand the fear of the LORD, and find the knowledge of God.*
>
> (Proverbs 2:3–5)

Stones are not broken except by an earnest use of the hammer, and the stone-breaker usually goes down on his knees. Use the hammer of diligence, and let the knee of prayer be exercised, too, and there is not a stony doctrine in Revelation that is useful for you to understand that will not fly into fragments under the exercise of prayer and faith. "Bene orasse est bene studuisse" was a wise sentence of Luther, which has so often been translated and quoted, "To have prayed well is to have studied well."

You can force your way through anything with the leverage of prayer. Thoughts and reasoning may be like the steel wedges that may open a way into truth, but prayer is the lever, the crowbar that forces open the iron chest of sacred mysteries so that we may get the treasure hidden in it for those who can force their way to reach it. *"Until now the kingdom of heaven suffereth violence, and the violent take it by force"* (Matthew 11:12). Take care that you work with the mighty implement of prayer, and nothing can stand against you.

Prayer Promotes Deeper Experience

We must not, however, stop there. We have applied the text to only one case. It is applicable to a hundred. We single out another. The saint may expect to discover deeper experience and to know more of the higher scriptural life by being much in prayer. There are different translations of our text, Jeremiah 33:3. One version says, *"I will show thee great and fortified things which thou knowest not."* Another reads, *"Great and reserved things which thou knowest not."* Now, all the developments of spiritual life are not similarly easy to attain.

There are the common experiences and feelings of repentance, faith, joy, and hope, which are enjoyed by the entire family. But there is an upper realm of rapture, of communion and conscious union with Christ, which is far from being the common dwelling place of believers. All believers see Christ, but all believers do not put their fingers into the prints of the nails or thrust their hand into His side. We do not have the high privilege of John to lean upon Jesus' chest, or of Paul to be caught up into the third heaven. In the ark of salvation, we find a lower, second, and third story—all are in the ark, but all do not abide on the same level. Most Christians, as to the river of experience, are only up to the ankles. Others have waded until the stream is up to their knees. Some find it chest-high. How few find it a river to swim in, the bottom of which they cannot touch!

Beloved friends, there are heights in experimental knowledge of the things of God that the eagle's discerning eye and philosophic thought have never seen. There are secret paths that the lion's reason and judgment have not as yet learned to travel. God alone can take us there, but the chariot in which He takes us up and the fiery steeds that pull that chariot are prevailing prayers. Prevailing prayer is victorious over the God of mercy: *"By his strength he had power with God: yea, he had power over the angel, and prevailed: he wept, and made supplication unto him: he found him* in Bethel, and there he spake with us" (Hosea 12:3–4).

Prevailing prayer takes the Christian to Carmel and enables him to cover heaven with clouds of blessing and earth with floods of mercy. Prevailing prayer bears the Christian aloft to Pisgah and shows him the reserved inheritance. It elevates him to Tabor and transfigures him until he is in the likeness of his Lord, until *"as he is, so are we in this world"* (1 John 4:17). If you want to reach something higher than ordinary groveling experience, look *"to the rock that is higher than [you]"* (Psalm 61:2); look with the eye of faith through the windows of unrelenting prayer. To grow in experience then, there must be much prayer.

Prayer Brings Deliverance

Have patience with me while I apply this verse to two or three more situations.

It is certainly true of one suffering under trial: if he waits upon God in much prayer, he will receive greater deliverances than he has ever dreamed of—*"great and mighty things, which thou knowest not."* Here is Jeremiah's testimony:

> *Thou drewest near in the day that I called upon thee: thou saidst, Fear not. O Lord, thou hast pleaded the causes of my soul; thou hast redeemed my life.*
> (Lamentations 3:57–58)

David's is the same: *"I called upon the LORD in distress: the LORD answered me, and set me in a large place....I will praise thee: for thou hast heard me, and art become my salvation"* (Psalm 118:5, 21). And again: *"Then they cried unto the LORD in their trouble, and he delivered them out of their distresses. And he led them forth by the right way, that they might go to a city of habitation"* (Psalm 107:6–7).

"My husband is dead," the poor woman cried to Elisha, *"...and the creditor is come to take unto him my two sons to be bondmen"* (2 Kings 4:1). She hoped that Elisha would possibly say, "What are your debts? I will pay them." Instead of that, he multiplied her oil and said, *"Go, sell the oil, and pay thy debt, and"* (what was the "and"?) *"live thou and thy children of the rest"* (v. 7). So often it will happen that God will not only help His people through the miry places along the way, so that they may just stand on the other side of the swamp, but He will bring them safely far ahead on the journey. It was a remarkable miracle when, in the midst of the storm, Jesus Christ came walking on the sea and the disciples received Him into the ship; not only was the sea calm, but *"immediately the ship was at the land whither they went"* (John 6:21).

That was a mercy over and above what they had asked. I sometimes hear people pray and make use of a quotation that is not in the Bible: "He is able to do exceeding abundantly above what we *can* ask or think." It is not written that way in the Bible. I do not know what we can ask or what we can think. But the Bible says, *"[He] is able to do exceeding abundantly above all **that we ask** or think"* (Ephesians 3:20, emphasis added).

Let us then, dear friends, when we are in great trial, simply say, "Now I am in prison. Like Jeremiah, I will pray, for I have God's command to do it. I will watch as he did, expecting that God will show me reserved mercies that I know nothing of at present." He will not merely bring His people through the battle, covering their heads in it, but He will bring them forth with banners waving, to divide the spoil with the strong and to claim their portion with the great (Isaiah 53:12). Expect great things of a God who gives such great promises as these.

Prayer Makes Us Useful

Again, here is encouragement for the worker. I am happy to say that you are probably doing something for Christ. Dear friend, wait upon God much in prayer, and you have the promise that He will do greater things for you than you know of. We do not know how much capacity for usefulness there may be in us. That donkey's jawbone lying there on the ground, what can it do? Nobody knows. But when it gets into Samson's hands, what can it not do? No one knows what it cannot do now that a Samson wields it. And you, friend, have often thought yourself to be as contemptible as that bone. You have said, "What can I do?" But when Christ by His Spirit grips you, what can you not do? Truly you may adopt Paul's words and say, *"I can do all things through Christ which strengtheneth me"* (Philippians 4:13).

However, do not depend on prayer without effort. In a certain school there was one girl, a very gracious, simple-hearted, trustful child, who knew the Lord. As usual, grace developed itself in the child according to the child's position. Her lessons were always prepared the best of any in the class. Another girl said to her, "How is it that your lessons are always so well done?" "I pray to God to help me to learn my lessons," she said. Well, thought the other, then I will do the same. The next morning when she stood up in the class, she knew nothing. When she was disgraced, she complained to the other girl, "Why, I prayed that God would help me learn my lesson, and I do not know any of it. What is the use of prayer?" "But did you sit down and try to learn it?" "Oh, no," she said, "I never looked at the book." "Ah," then said the other, "I asked God to help me to learn my lesson, but then I sat down to study and kept at it until I knew it well. I learned it easily because my earnest desire, which I had expressed to God, was, 'Help me to be diligent in endeavoring to do my duty.'"

So is it with some who come to prayer meetings and pray and then fold their arms and go away, hoping that God's work will go on. This is like the woman who sang, "Fly abroad, thou mighty Gospel," but did not put a penny in the plate. Her friend touched her and said, "But how can it fly if you don't give it wings to fly with?"

There are many who appear to be very mighty in prayer, wondrous in supplications, but they require God to do what they can do themselves. Therefore, God does nothing at all for them. "I shall leave my camel untied," said an Arab once to Mohammed, "and trust to providence." "Tie it up tight," said Mohammed, "and then trust to providence." So you who say, "I will pray and trust my church, or my class, or my work to God's goodness," may rather hear the voice of experience and wisdom that says, "Do your best. Work as if all rested on your toil, as if your own arm would bring your salvation. When you have done all, cast yourself on Him without whom it is in vain to rise up early and to sit up late, and to eat the bread of anxiety (Psalm 127:2), and if He gives you success, give Him the praise."

Comfort for Intercessors

I want to point out that this promise ought to prove useful for the comfort of those who are intercessors for others. You who are calling upon God to save your children, to bless your neighbors, to remember your husband or your wife in mercy, may find assurance from this: *"I will...show thee great and mighty things, which thou knowest not."* A celebrated minister in the last century, one Mr. Bailey, was the child of a godly mother. This mother had almost ceased to pray for her husband, who was a man of a most ungodly character and a bitter persecutor. The mother prayed for her boy, and while he was still eleven or twelve years of age, eternal mercy met with him. So sweetly instructed was the child in the things of the kingdom of God that the mother requested him—and for some time he always did so—to conduct family prayer in the house. Morning and evening this little one laid open the Bible. Though the father would not deign to stop for the family prayer, on one occasion he was rather curious, so he stopped on the other side of the door to listen. God blessed the prayer of his own child under thirteen years of age to his conversion. The mother might well have read my text with streaming eyes and said, "Yes, Lord, You have shown me great and mighty things which I knew not. You have not only saved my boy, but through my boy, You have brought my husband to the truth."

You cannot guess how greatly God will bless you. Only go and stand at His door, for you cannot tell what is in reserve for you. If you do not beg at all, you will get nothing. But if you beg, He may not only give you, as it were, the bones and leftover meat, but He may say to the servant at His table, "Take that choice meat, and set it before the poor man."

Ruth went to glean. She expected to get a few good ears, but Boaz said, *"Let her glean even among the sheaves, and reproach her not"* (Ruth 2:15). Furthermore, he said to her, *"At mealtime come thou hither, and eat of the bread, and dip thy morsel in the vinegar"* (v. 14). She found a husband where she only expected to find a handful of barley. So in prayer for others, God may give us such mercies that we will be astounded at them, since we expected but little. Hear what is said of Job, and learn its lesson:

> *The LORD said...my servant Job shall pray for you: for him will I accept: lest I deal with you after your folly, in that ye have not spoken of me the thing which is right, like my servant Job....And the LORD turned the captivity of Job, when he prayed for his friends: also the LORD gave Job twice as much as he had before.*
>
> (Job 42:7–8, 10)

Instructions for Those Seeking Salvation

Finally, some of you are seeking for your own conversion. God has quickened you to solemn prayer about your own souls. You are not content to go to hell; you want heaven. You want to be washed in the precious blood. You want eternal life.

Dear friends, I ask you to take this text—God Himself speaks it to you: *"Call unto me, and I will answer thee, and show thee great and mighty things, which thou knowest not."* Take God at His Word at once. Get home, go into your room, shut the door, and try Him. Young man, I say, try the Lord. Young woman, prove Him. See whether He is true or not. If God is true, you cannot seek mercy at His hands through Jesus Christ and receive a negative reply. He must open mercy's gate to you who knock with all your heart, for His own promise and character bind Him to it.

May God help you, believing in Christ Jesus, to cry aloud unto Him, and His answer of peace is already on the way to meet you. You will hear Him say, "[Your] *sins, which are many, are forgiven"* (Luke 7:47).

The Lord bless you for His love's sake. Amen.

OTHER POWERFUL $\mathcal{B}$ OOKS

from Whitaker House

Morning by Morning
Charles H. Spurgeon

As the day begins, it is fitting to open our eyes and hearts to our Creator. Morning devotions anchor the soul so that it is less likely to stumble on the day's journey. Spurgeon said that to rush from bed to business without first talking with God is as foolish as forgetting to bathe or dress. A day of grace begins with time spent alone with God.

ISBN: 0-88368-645-7 • Trade • 384 pages

Evening by Evening
Charles H. Spurgeon

In the quiet of the evening, God is ready to speak to your heart. Are you prepared to hear His voice? Combining Scripture with an inspiring and comforting message for each day, Charles Spurgeon shepherds you into intimate communication with the Father like you've never known before. Each evening you will find solace in God's Word.

ISBN: 0-88368-646-5 • Trade • 384 pages